ROBERT ASHLEY

AMERICAN

Composers

A list of books in the series appears at the end of this book.

Robert Ashley

Kyle Gann

UNIVERSITY OF ILLINOIS PRESS
Urbana, Chicago, and Springfield

∞ This book is printed
on acid-free paper.

Cataloging-in-Publication Data available
from the Library of Congress
ISBN 978-0-252-03549-4 (cloth : alk.)
ISBN 978-0-252-07887-3 (paper : alk.)
ISBN 978-0-252-09456-9 (ebook)

CONTENTS

LIST OF ILLUSTRATIONS vii

PREFACE ix

1. Oh, How We Misunderstand: Introduction 1
2. The Vessel of the Eternal Present: The Early Years 7
3. When Slow Starts to Mean Something, We Crave Fast: The ONCE Years 23
4. Incredibly Slowly Our View Begins to Slide: The Mills College Years 46
5. I'm Not the Same Person That I Used to Be: *Perfect Lives* 57
6. Who Could Speak If Every Word Had Meaning?: *Atalanta (Acts of God)* 77
7. If You Have to Ask You Can't Afford One: *Now Eleanor's Idea* 87
8. One Thing Follows the Next and I Just Do It: *Dust*, *Celestial Excursions*, *Concrete*, and Smaller Pieces 110

CHRONOLOGICAL LIST OF WORKS BY ROBERT ASHLEY 131

NOTES 135

SELECTED BIBLIOGRAPHY 143

DISCOGRAPHY 145

INDEX 147

ILLUSTRATIONS

PHOTOS

Following page 56

Ted Hariton and Robert Ashley, ca. 1938

Anne Ward, Diane, and Robert Ashley, ca. 1948

Diane, Anne Ward, and Nancy Ashley, ca. 1948

ONCE Group and Judson Dance Theater members, ca. 1965

Alvin Lucier, Robert Ashley, and Anne Koren, 1975

Robert Ashley, New York, 1980

Robert Ashley in *Atalanta (Acts of God)*, 1985

Atalanta (Acts of God) at the Centre Georges Pompidou, Paris, 1982

Robert Ashley in *Concrete*, 2009

Robert Ashley in *Dust*, 2008

Robert Ashley in *Celestial Excursions*, 2003

Robert Ashley, Flagstaff, Arizona, 2009

FIGURES

1. A page from *in memoriam . . . CRAZY HORSE (symphony)* 35

2. A page from *Foreign Experiences* 59

3. Symmetry among four Ashley works 89

TABLES

1. Duration and tempo in the four operas of *Now Eleanor's Idea* 88

2. Vocal pitches in *Improvement* 91

3. Rhythms in *Outcome Inevitable* 112

PREFACE

I MAY HAVE FIRST SEEN THE NAME ROBERT ASHLEY in David Cope's book *New Directions in Music*, which I read in high school and which describes his notorious piece *The Wolfman* in the "Anti-Music" chapter: "The recording of this work . . . constitutes ear annihilation to the uninitiated."[1] I also read about Ashley in *Source* magazine in college libraries and found out more from Michael Nyman's 1974 book *Experimental Music: Cage and Beyond*. The first music of his that I heard was the piece *Purposeful Lady Slow Afternoon*, on the 1971 Mainstream recording of the Sonic Arts Union. Back then I used to hang out for hours with my friend Marcus in record stores in Dallas, our home town. It often happened that Marcus and I would light on the same seductive record, of which there was only one copy in the bin, and we more or less took turns letting each other buy such finds. In this case I won. We took the record to my parents' house and listened, before dinner, to Alvin Lucier's experimental and rather abstract *Vespers*. Then Ashley's *Purposeful Lady Slow Afternoon* came on. A hiss of white noise started up, and Cynthia Liddell's husky voice began hesitantly reciting:

> I remember he tried to put his gum in my mouth.
> I remember it felt afterwards like my mouth was open for the whole time.
> I remember my mouth felt stretched afterwards.[2]

This transfixed our attention, and we stopped talking. We made it, I recall, as far as the line

> I remember one time he put his finger between my legs and got it wet and tried to put that finger in my mouth.[3]

By now, Marcus and I were staring at each other with saucer-wide eyes. I whipped the record off the turntable, and we agreed that we could finish listening to that one after my parents went to bed. Which we certainly did. We were used to contemporary music's being an esoteric, even nerdy pursuit, one that made us seem merely odd and bookish to our peers; suddenly we learned that it could be a more vivid and spicier world than we had imagined.

From that moment, Ashley was a fixed point on my radar screen. A couple of other recordings turned up: *She Was a Visitor* on Odyssey, *in memoriam . . . Crazy Horse (symphony)* on Advance. I remember, at age eighteen, attending a reception that the wild-man composer Jerry Hunt gave for John Cage when the latter made a Dallas appearance; Jerry babbled on in his lightning-fast way about his friend "B'bashley," and I was excited to meet someone who not only knew Ashley but did so well enough to call him by his nickname; this was years before *Perfect Lives* appeared. As a graduate teaching assistant at Northwestern University, I took over a professor's American music course for a couple of weeks and played *Purposeful Lady* for the class. A male student, incensed, stormed out (the girls in class had loved it) and complained to the dean, who called me into his office and made me assure him that the piece indeed had socially redeeming value. (The next day a pretty undergrad who had skipped class yelled to me, "Kyle! I hear you played a piece in class called 'Blowjob'!")

Then, on October 24, 1979, Ashley came to campus, by invitation of my raffishly progressive composition teacher, Peter Gena. That afternoon Ashley gave a talk to the composition students and described how he composed using templates. Afterward, sensing my enthusiasm, the chair of the music theory department asked me if I had understood anything Ashley was talking about. I answered, "Of course"—which was only a slight bragging exaggeration. That night, Ashley and "Blue" Gene Tyranny gave the first complete performance of *Private Parts*, the opera that would soon be renamed *Perfect Lives*. Ashley liked to sip vodka while performing, and as chief student go-fer, one of my jobs was to run to Desplaines (since Evanston was a dry town) and procure some. My other responsibility, during the performance, was to sit backstage and turn the index cards containing the opera's text over in front of a camera so Ashley could read them on a video monitor onstage. From the shadows in which I heard without seeing, I was absolutely swallowed up by the music: it was cheeky, uninhibited, yet erudite and magnificently calm. I was enchanted. I had learned, to recycle Ashley's words from that evening, that "short ideas repeated massage the brain."

Since that night thirty-odd years ago, I have considered Ashley one of the greatest twentieth-century composers. As subsequent works appeared—*Atalanta*, *Improvement: Don Leaves Linda*, *Dust*, *Celestial Excursions*—I have come to think of him as one of the most profoundly imaginative and innovative composers of any period, a Monteverdi for our own time. As I have had the great privilege to interview him over the years, to write about his work in the *Village Voice* and elsewhere, to socialize with him, and to sit in bars as he expounded his counterintuitive theories about the world, I have found him an unceasing font of inspiration, an artist absolutely contemptuous of the world's approval or disapproval, a seeker after a vision from whose pursuit he would not swerve in the slightest, no matter how discouraging the institutional response. I have never left him without feeling energized and emboldened by his artistic courage. I have known hundreds of composers but not found another I could compare to him in those respects.

I have to further say that Ashley's has got to be the most remarkable mind I've ever encountered, and that's saying something. To enter his world is to enter a labyrinth, like a house you thought you'd basically explored, but every day you find another wing, an attic, basements beneath basements, until you lose any confidence that you can guess its extent. Over and over again I'd ask a question, he'd start to answer, then he'd say, "Wait, I have to tell you an anecdote first," but understanding that anecdote would require backing up to a previous story and introducing a couple of new characters, and so it would go, anecdote after nested anecdote, and half an hour later he would give the answer along with all of the previous information required for the answer to make sense. And he'd never lose sight of the answer he was aiming for. Like his operas, Ashley's life is built up hierarchically in layers upon cascading layers of associations, and to leave out one person or event threatens to render the whole ultimately enigmatic. Every interview brought its surprises and overarching new insights, until I quit expecting to stop being surprised.

Ashley is extremely articulate when explaining his music in print, and many times I thought his published writings were sufficient background for discussing one of his pieces with him, but mentioning it to him would bring up a whole other set of associations, and I'd realize what he'd published was only the tip of an iceberg. Though he was seventy-nine or eighty when I conducted the interviews for this book (2009–10), his memory was astonishing; he'd have to hunt for proper names as would any of us over fifty, but he would outline the theoretical background of a piece he wrote in 1963 as easily, and in as much detail, as he would one written in 2003. I have cross-checked his version of events wherever possible and rarely caught him in a mistake. As though he had mastered Giordano Bruno's art of memory, which he loves so much, he seemed to be looking at pictures of his life in his head. Discussing some insight or conversation he'd had in 1967, he'd say things like, "And then that Saturday morning around 10 A.M., I was sitting in my studio." Of course, I couldn't verify the accuracy of these specifics, but they sounded convincing. The amount of detailed material he could keep in his head at once, ready for use, impressed me greatly.

And his external organization is as immaculate as the internal. I'd ask about the musical structure of an opera he wrote over twenty years ago, and he'd walk over to the piano and play through the chords for me, then hand me the information on a piece of paper that happened to be lying there. Certainly he's a creative genius, but I also got the impression that he's a genius in the most vernacular sense of the word: an IQ through the roof and an encyclopedic memory, a supersized brain with every piston firing and connections intact. That's not true of every great musician, let alone every hard-drinking, octogenarian great musician.

Over the course of two summers, Ashley gave me (and sometimes my black-metal guitarist son, Bernard) about thirty hours' worth of interview time, in addition to answering a relentless stream of queries and correcting my errors patiently and meticulously. This is my official opportunity to thank Bob for his generosity and, even more, for his inspiration. Were the book to never bring me another scrap of benefit, the opportunity to spend so many mornings and afternoons talking to him will have been well worth the work I put into it. It has been one of the great experiences of my life.

In addition, I'd like to thank Mimi Johnson for letting me impinge on her time and hospitality, and Joan La Barbara, Thomas Buckner, Tom Hamilton, Jacqueline Humbert, David Rosenboom, and especially "Blue" Gene Tyranny for granting me long interviews and in some cases loaning me materials. I thank Anne Ward (née Ashley) and her husband Patrick Conlon for a delightful afternoon of family stories. I thank Pauline Waters of the Ann Arbor Historical Society, Karma Pippin at the Special Collections Library of Mills College, and the helpful staff of Special Collections at the University of Michigan. I owe very special thanks to my brother-in-law Sean Cook, who lent considerable time, his expertise as a Michigan real estate appraiser, and his knack for sweet-talking bureaucrats to help me trace Ashley's family information at the Washtenaw County Clerk's Office. I thank my editor at the University of Illinois Press, Laurie Matheson, for letting me go with what may have seemed like a wild idea. I thank my anonymous readers of the manuscript for catching mistakes and motivating some worthwhile rewriting. I thank the National Endowment for the Humanities for a grant that allowed me to begin work. And, as always, I thank my wife, Nancy, for her unwavering support.

This book is merely an introduction; each of Ashley's major works deserves one at least as long. Since I have been limited here in the kinds of strictly musical information I can convey, I include more technical examples from Ashley's works on my Web site, at http://www.kylegann.com/Ashley.html, to which I refer the reader for more in-depth information. But I hope this book will start the ball rolling and convince the uninformed and skeptical that Ashley is one of the most original, important, and compelling composers of this postmodern era.

ROBERT ASHLEY

I Oh, How We Misunderstand

Introduction

All the world's people revel in oral sex
We had to stop asking the question except the British
We don't do it OK you don't do it and we know why
Nobody takes a bath Jane Austen didn't take a bath
She wrote her ass off but she didn't take a bath
Mr. Darcy never took a bath Disraeli never took a bath
The whole place smelled to high heaven whole
Cults jumped on boats to the New World they knew
Something was amiss Charles Dickens never took a bath
Until he met Mark Twain who kidded him so bad about stinking
That he took a bath he hadn't seen his own legs in 15 years
The fucker almost drowned End of insert back to scene ten

—*Foreign Experiences*, Act 1

***THAT'S* OPERA?** The voices chant ecstatically on one pitch, echoing and overlapping in almost unintelligible profusion. The piano beats out a sporadic, dissonant pointillism, though the background electronics reinforce an immobile tonality, a frozen ritual, an undistinguishable fragment of eternity. Each of four scenes is a few seconds over eighteen minutes in length, and all are at the same tempo, a peculiar formal symmetry given the seemingly frantic outpouring of words from someone's babbling subconscious. Where do these ideas come from? How can these voices jabber the same non sequiturs in unison?

Robert Ashley's works do not fit the profile of what people generally think of as opera. In his pieces people sing in a style that resembles speech, within a small pitch range and with pitch and stress inflections based on speech; one of Ashley's guiding premises is that speech is itself music, that the melody of speech patterns can be *composed*. Plots are rarely evident in his works, or, rather, if there's a background plot (and several of his operas share one overarching background plot), you can't necessarily reconstruct it from the text. His works are made not for the stage but for television. As he told me in a 1991 interview,

> I put my pieces in television format because I believe that's really the only possibility for music. I hate to say that. But I don't believe that this recent fashion of American composers trying to imitate stage opera from Europe means anything. It's not going to go anywhere. We don't have any tradition. If you've never been to the Paris Opera, never been to La Scala, never been to the Met more than once, we're talking primitivism. How can you write the pieces if you've never been there? It's like Eskimos playing baseball. It's crazy! It's nuts! It's superstition. The form is related to the architecture. La Scala's architecture doesn't mean anything to us. We don't go there. We stay home and watch television. We go there like we go to the Statue of Liberty, but it's from another time, like the pyramids.[1]

The theorist Arthur Sabatini has sidestepped the terminology issue by dubbing Ashley's works "performance novels," in other words, expansions of the "idea of story-telling modeled on the technology of the electronic media."[2] Then again, as Ashley once exclaimed in good humor to a music critic, "Well, if I say it's opera, it's opera! Who's running this show, anyway?"[3]

In fact, it is a thesis of this book that Ashley is not only an opera composer but the greatest opera composer of the last half-century and the most innovative opera composer since at least Harry Partch, if not Monteverdi. The word *opera* literally means "works," and the genre originally took this name in the seventeenth century because it was a fusion of different media: music, text, scenery, and action. In this sense Ashley is a quintessentially operatic composer in the same way Richard Wagner was. Like Wagner, he writes his own texts (one hesitates to call them librettos in the conventional sense). As with Wagner's texts, Ashley's are poetic; they are, in fact, epic poems. Like the ancient epics of Homer and Hesiod, they are made of episodes and are meant to be heard while being read aloud—which is how we experience them in his operas. Moreover, it is thought that ancient epics were sung and accompanied by music, so Ashley's operas represent a technologically updated revival of an ancient tradition. More than anyone else, though, Ashley remade opera from the ground up as an American form, not oratorical but vernacular, not for the stage but for television, not originating in musical notation but in speech and electronic technology.

Ashley's operas overload the senses. They are mesmerizing. They are as familiar as a conversation at the local diner yet sometimes (equally) incomprehensible. They have a Buddhistic flavor, written as they are from the standpoint of eternity (*sub specie aeternitatis*, to use the classical phrase). They embody overarching theories about the history of humanity. Like the novels of James Joyce and Henry

Miller, they do not—as evident above—shy away from sex and profanity. They are at times riotously funny. In source material they range from Renaissance occultism to Hindu cosmology to the financial pages of the *Wall Street Journal* to boogie-woogie to country and western music to recent research on the evolution of the brain to cult fan magazines. They erase the lines between classical music, pop music, and the avant-garde. They are a world unto themselves, playful, absorbing, dazzling, thought-provoking, infinitely quotable.

Yet—or, perhaps, predictably—Ashley remains a somewhat marginalized figure in the "serious music" world, and one vastly misunderstood. How can someone whose primary creative act is to talk, and then write down that talking, be considered a composer? His insouciant-sounding texts are more carefully constructed than they seem. Ashley is highly unusual in the extent to which his works are collaborative, dependent on the art of the core group of musicians he's worked with for thirty years. He doesn't fit the pattern of the all-determining classical composer. Only a handful of his works are written in standard musical notation. His scores don't look like what people think of as music. His documentation consists of long texts divided into lines, chord charts, and MIDI files, and often the final documentation is the recording itself, produced in his Tribeca, New York, studio. He doesn't have any known pattern in common with any other composer. He has blazed an independent path, devoid of models. The classical music world has no idea what to do with him. Experts on conventional opera frequently don't even recognize his name. The pop world is equally oblivious. Yet to his broad cult following—those who discover his music, don't care about categories, and get irresistibly drawn into his narrative wheels within wheels—he is *the* postmodern opera composer. There really is no one else.

Because of the unconventionality of Ashley's methods, his achievement as a composer has been greatly underrated. It's true that he leaves "Blue" Gene Tyranny free to invent some of the gorgeous piano textures for his operas, and since that's what people hear on the surface, it leads some to think that Ashley's not really composing his own music. It's a classical music hang-up—one might as well say the same of Duke Ellington, a predecessor Ashley acknowledges: "It's like when Duke Ellington sets up his band. It's a collection of characters, and Ellington understands it that way. Ellington's music is not written in the way a symphony, which can be played by anybody, is written. If you pull out a player in Ellington's band, you have to rewrite the part. *Perfect Lives* is based on that model."[4] I once asked Tyranny if he felt that Ashley's operas should be considered multiple-author works, and he quickly answered, "No. I think my part of it was akin to scenic design. The whole conception/structural thing is all Robert's."[5]

What's also little realized is how remarkably, even fanatically, structured Ashley's operas are, with types of structure that only a composer with big ideas could imagine. The ecstatic outpouring of words sounds improvisatory, but look closely and you'll notice that all the scenes in one opera have the same number of beats, that two different operas may have the same number of beats and same-sized sections, or that the drone pitches the singers are chanting on spell out an overarching tone row that also runs through the work at other speeds. The discipline to create such free-sounding streams of consciousness within obsessively ordered forms requires amazing forethought and winnowing and reshaping, and Ashley is as rigorous about following his own rules as any sixteenth-century composer of intricate canons. In college, he absorbed J. S. Bach as an important model. No one else has ever applied to opera the kinds of structure that Ashley has invented, and so few know where to look for his purely musical innovations.

We commonly think of great composers as revealing their talent early in life and developing their style incrementally. Some have stunning early successes, as Igor Stravinsky did with *The Firebird.* Others start out more imitatively and gradually find their voice, as Beethoven did at thirty-five with the *Eroica* Symphony. One conundrum of Robert Ashley is that at age forty-eight—pretty late in life by composers' standards—he suddenly emerged as a full-blown genius of opera. Before 1978 he had possessed some profile as an avant-garde composer, but mainly as part of a crowd: he was one of the composers associated with the wild and crazy ONCE festivals, which made the unlikely college town of Ann Arbor, Michigan, an international center for new music in the 1960s. Then, in 1979, *Perfect Lives* appeared, and with it a whole new conception of technology-driven music theater.

Many of Ashley's subsequent large works—*Atalanta, Your Money My Life Goodbye, Music Word Fire and I Would Do It Again (Coo Coo), Yellow Man with Heart with Wings,* the four operas of *Now Eleanor's Idea*—came from *Perfect Lives.* This is true in an unusually literal way, since to some extent these works all had their narrative origin in the hectic climax of the whimsical plot for *Perfect Lives.* It's somewhat like the way a novelist keeps bringing back the same characters in different novels—Robertson Davies and John Le Carré are examples—but it applies here to historical constructs and musical structures as well. Of course, *Perfect Lives* also came from two decades' worth of Ashley's previous works, such as the infamous *The Wolfman* and the more ambitious *That Morning Thing*—but this is a more difficult proposition to demonstrate, and doing so is one of the challenges of this book. Nothing in the first forty-eight years of Ashley's life made it look likely that he would create a new, well-defined form of electronic opera, though in hindsight links are not difficult to find. The inspiration for *Perfect Lives* is the point that divides Ashley's creative life cleanly in half. Before 1978 he was a visible but fairly typical 1960s avant-gardist; after that date, he appeared, like Monteverdi, as simultaneously the revolutionary of opera and also its master, transcending in one athletic leap the milieu from which his aesthetic developed. Specifically, the pre-1978 music gives us little hint of Ashley's subsequent magical verbal expertise with phrases, sentences, and entire paragraphs. To quote a line reused in several of Ashley's works, How is that possible? Rendering this transformation intelligible is no small feat. But we must do it in order to understand how Ashley seemed to jump a century or so ahead in the history of music theater.

Before I proceed to biography, allow me a cautionary word about the reception of Ashley's operas. The main focus of this book is the nine operas spanning from *Perfect Lives* to *Concrete*, twenty-five to thirty hours of text-dense music (and perhaps I should throw in the briefer yet stellar *Your Money My Life Goodbye*). It's an astoundingly imaginative and engaging body of music, but Ashley remains as controversial today as he has always been. Many love him; some can't stand him. First of all, I think one misses some streak of Ashley's genius if one fails to note a tongue-in-cheek aspect to his music theater—not that he's putting anything over on the audience, but he's often putting something over on his characters. As he says of the people in one work, "Everybody's crazy." I would characterize his genre as sacro-philosophico-comedic. Streams of philosophical ideas, both serious and absurd, course through the operas, and they sometimes crescendo to a cathartic level of spiritual release, but the characters are somewhat humorously self-aware and self-effacing, Buddhistic in their willingness to accept events as they come. Ashley's profundity and his laid-back cynicism complement and need each other. The too-literal listener may sometimes be frustrated. The fan willing to enter into the personal mythology will be delighted by layers and layers of new meaning.

In addition, let me confess that I have not myself consistently found Ashley's works easy to approach. *Perfect Lives* I loved from the get-go, and then *Improvement: Don Leaves Linda* disappointed me because I wanted it to be like *Perfect Lives*; today I consider *Improvement* slightly the more perfect work. Much of *Foreign Experiences* I found chaotic and off-putting until I read carefully through the text a couple of times and learned to love its raw, spitting grandeur. *Dust*, so disconcertingly vulnerable and harmonically simple, knocked me off my feet on the first listen; I'm still coming to terms with the conceptual complexity of *Atalanta* after twenty-five years. Like John Cage's and Karlheinz Stockhausen's, Ashley's is a wide-ranging, unfettered imagination unafraid to wander outside the boundaries of what most consider art. Some people can't handle him. But every one of these works has come to impress me more and more upon closer analysis, and affection, whether immediate or gradual, has always been the result. There's a lot in Ashley to entice the ear at once, but when it isn't initially evident, I recommend immersion and patience. As the narrator in *Improvement* says about Linda's actions, "Oh, how we misunderstand."

2 The Vessel of the Eternal Present

The Early Years

TO A REMARKABLE EXTENT, ROBERT ASHLEY is the unofficial token composer of Ann Arbor, Michigan. It's a college town; the University of Michigan has a distinguished music department, and many famous composers have taught there. Ashley never has, but he was born in Ann Arbor, and to some extent he thinks of his operas as drawn from the melody of the distinctive southeastern Michigan accent. Ashley earned his bachelor's degree from the University of Michigan and later worked on a doctorate there, which he never completed. Afterward, though, he spent the early part of his creative life in Ann Arbor as co-founder and co-director of the ONCE festivals. On and off, the town remained his center of activities for thirty-nine years. In the operas, he refers to it as "Headquarters."

In the early twentieth century, Ann Arbor's principal industry was milling, followed by light manufacturing, furniture making, piano building, brewing, gas fixture making, and rug making.[1] The university was an important economic base: between 1900 and 1920 the student population more than doubled, rising from 3,441 to 9,401. The area was conservative overall, and Washtenaw County was one of the few in Michigan to vote for Herbert Hoover in the 1932 election, 15,368 votes to 12,552. The area was hard hit by the Depression—the number of families on relief soared from 162 to 405 between 1931 and 1933, and the unemployment rate would hit 20 percent—but it recovered more quickly than most towns in the state, in part due to the buoying effects of the university.[2]

There Robert Reynolds Ashley was born March 28, 1930. His paternal grandfather, Alvah J. Ashley, had come to Ann Arbor in 1893 from the town of Bay City to the north; Ashley thinks his family had worked there in the timber business. Alvah (his first name is sometimes listed in public documents without the *h*) brought with him his wife Sarah Ashley (1857–1936) and his sons Ward J. (1883–1950) and Alvah J. Ashley (1886–1961); the latter was called not Alvah or Junior but for some reason Cy, short for Cyrus. Alvah Senior was listed in the Ann Arbor city directories of the time as a clerk, and he seems to have died in 1908 or 1909.[3] Ward is first listed in 1900 as a messenger for the Post Office; on January 1, 1902, at age seventeen, he started a job there as a dispatch clerk and worked there for a total of fifty years. Following Alvah's death, Sarah and her sons lived in various apartments until Ward, in 1914, bought them a house at 702 Ingalls Street, a block north of the present University of Michigan campus. Ironically, given his son's ultimate profession, Ward became deaf in his late twenties, a victim of (Ashley thinks) a streptococcus epidemic that tended to cause deafness in men. Able to lip-read and barely register loud speech, he would figure in a story in Ashley's opera *Dust*.

Meanwhile, in 1923 Nancy Reynolds (1899–1996) came from the tiny crossroads of Indian Mound in Stewart County, Tennessee, to either Ann Arbor or Detroit, driving up in a Model T with a few friends.[4] She got a job in the Post Office there and met Ward, already deaf and sixteen years her senior, but with a stable job. Ward and Nancy married on July 18, 1927. This seemed like a better life than the impoverished tobacco farm back in Stewart County, so at some point Nancy's mother, Floy E. Lewis Reynolds (1874–1960), widow of Thomas Mann Reynolds (1869–1908), came to Ann Arbor as well with Nancy's siblings, Ann LaRee, Rosalie, Leon, Thomas, and Willard. Ashley grew up close to this grandmother, whom he called Mama. As he would later say of her in *Foreign Experiences*,

> I
> Grew up with my grandmother, who liked to drink,
> So, we had this thing between us, like Everybody
> Has with Somebody. We liked to drink together.
> We did this for years and years. Get drunk together.
> She'd be sixty and I'd be five, and we'd get drunk together.
> Then we sort of broke up, when I had to go to school.
> To learn not to think.[5]

In "Empire," a story from his opera *Atalanta*, Ashley further mentions that the beer they drank was always warm and that he never came to trust people who drink their beer cold. Ashley never learned, though, what had brought Nancy to Ann Arbor. He says his mother would never discuss anything personal and, if asked anything about her courtship days or early life, would simply change the subject. Nancy's siblings were the family Robert Ashley grew up with, and Willard (1908–68), the loquacious family storyteller, would become a major character in *Atalanta*.

Starting in 1920, Alvah the younger (Cy) is listed as a grocer; he and his wife Bessie operated a store at the corner of Dewey Avenue and South State Street. (Ashley's sister Anne Ward remembers that because of the grocery store, the kids never lacked for basics like chewing gum during World War II.) In 1926 and 1927, respectively, Ward and Alvah bought adjoining plots at 706 Dewey Street and 702 Dewey Street; Ashley would spend the first five years of his life at the former address. According to the composer, Ward—who had an interest in abolitionism and knew the local sites of the Underground Railroad—didn't much care for Bessie, who was the daughter of the racist sheriff of Dearborn County. Robert was born in 1930, and his sisters, Diane and Anne Ward (the latter always called by both names), in 1932 and 1937, respectively. In 1935 Ward borrowed $1,700 from the Ann Arbor Savings Bank and moved his growing family two miles south to a farmhouse on a two-acre lot at 2667 Packard Road, in Pittsfield Township, where they would live for ten years. Young Bob felt isolated in this quasi-rural setting, although he did have a friend his age across Kimberly Road, Theodore (Ted) Hariton, whose exotic Jewish mother would become the model for Linda in *Improvement*. Ted would grow up to become a gynecologist in California and have a number of celebrity patients from the television and film worlds and also would serve as a medical consultant for the popular television show *Dallas*. He and Ashley remained in lifelong, if intermittent, touch.[6]

In 1945 the Ward Ashley family moved back into town and lived at 849 Brookwood Place in Ann Arbor, just off Packard Street (a long diagonal road) and only a couple of blocks from the Dewey Avenue address. Ashley's family was nominally Methodist—"They *said* they went to the Methodist Church," as he puts it—but he remembers going only on Christmas. Once, his mother put him in a Holy Roller Bible camp to get him out of the way in the summer, and he was shocked to see people, as he put it, "rolling in the dust for Jesus"—a line that appears in *Perfect Lives*.[7] In addition to the First Methodist Church, Ward belonged to the Golden Rule Lodge, the Free and Accepted Masons, and the Zal Gaz Grotto,[8] a Freemasons' social club that still exists. Anne Ward insists, though, that her father's involvement in such activities was minimal at best.

Living on Brookwood, Ashley attended the University High School, part of a system of experimental laboratory schools that gave students an unusual level of freedom; it existed to provide teaching experience for University of Michigan graduate students in education. (The schools were discontinued in the 1960s as too "elitist.") Ashley was popular in high school, captain of the football team and president of the student council. He himself is, in fact, the model for Donnie, captain of the football team, in *Perfect Lives*. One of his friends would become the model for Ed Strapping in that opera. Another, a girl he liked to drink with because she had the key to her father's liquor cabinet, was abandoned on the church steps by the man who was supposed to marry her; in *Perfect Lives* her nickname is Snowdrift.

On April 27, 1950, Ashley's father, aged sixty-six, dropped dead at the Post Office from a coronary thrombosis. Despite the illness that caused his deafness, his obituary in the *Ann Arbor News* stated that he had never missed a day of work until he suffered a heart attack in 1946.[9] (One must credit some fraction of Ashley's lifelong stick-to-itiveness about his music to this reliable role model.) Anne Ward remembers that after this, Robert took over as head of the family and exhibited an authoritarian streak. She wanted to attend public school with her friends rather than attend University High School, and she had to beg him for permission. Ashley's robust mother would live forty-six more years to the august age of ninety-seven, the last surviving family member of her generation.

What first drew Ashley to music during the Brookwood days remains a mystery to him. "When I was a kid, there was just the radio," he told me. "I didn't see a person play the piano live until I was 15 years old."[10] That person was local jazz pianist Dickie Johnson, who played with the Johnny Harberd Orchestra, a group organized by the Post Office custodian, who invited Ward to come hear them. The younger Ashley followed Johnson around to watch him play local gigs and years later found him reduced to working on a sanitation truck.[11] Ashley also remembers owning 78-rpm records of pianists Meade Lux Lewis and Albert Ammons and a record with "the Boss of the Blues," singer Joe Turner; he listened to them until they were practically worn out. His Tennessee grandmother Floy had also once played "porch violin" in the style that Bill Monroe would later transform into bluegrass. As a teenager Ashley formed a boogie-woogie band, imitating Lewis, Ammons, Nat King Cole, and other pop music greats of the day. This early love would re-emerge in the great hymn to boogie-woogie at the center of "The Bar," the central scene of *Perfect Lives*:

> In other words,
> Keep moving is Rodney's [horoscope] chart.
> And he interprets that to mean

The money Baby spent
    On lessons at the music store
Will not ensure her place
    Among the greats of boogie-woogie . . . or even,
Get her playing at the bar.
    Happy she is, the traveling
Salesmen say,
    But boogie-woogie
She is not.
    Thirty lessons guaranteed to merge
The left hand with the right.
    In one ear and out the other hand,
Across the great divide.
    Some got it and some don't,
She says at night. . . .
    I got it, Rodney's Baby says,
Boogie-woogie all the way . . .

CCEE CCGG CCBB CCGG
CCEE CCGG CCBB CCGG
    Always.
Boogie-woogie is the vessel of the eternal present.
    That's the only way to use that word.[12]

Ashley also studied with a "horrible" piano teacher, who, as he remembers it, spent five years trying to teach him to play the Norwegian composer Christian Sinding's light popular classic *Rustle of Spring*. "I could never learn it, all those arpeggios, I could never do that stuff at all. I would go to her house Thursday afternoons after school for, I don't know, a half-hour, and then I'd go home. *Rustle of Spring* is sort of the emblem of trying to learn music."

Between the ages of fifteen and eighteen, Ashley delivered ice to make money. These were the days in which the old-fashioned icebox was being replaced by the modern refrigerator, and Ashley notes that his customers included not the middle class, who were switching, but the poor—who couldn't afford a refrigerator—and the very rich, who possessed fancy mahogany iceboxes built into their pantries, too cherished to replace.

"[T]he idea of the music being about the people who make it," Ashley said in a 1984 interview, "is a fairly new idea, but it's also a very important idea, and it's becoming more important all the time."[13] Accordingly, stories about Ashley's youth crop up in his later operas, and he swears that every word is true (though he will concede the occasional exaggeration). In *Dust* (1998) there's a story about a friend of Ashley's, a "hoodlum," who was very smart and obsessed with theosophy and who wanted to marry Ashley's sister Diane (which he eventually did). Ashley portrays himself as a "sissy":

> I don't like fighting. And I'm no good at it.
> I always get a big one.
> And there's like a lump on my face for a couple of days.
> I always lose. . . .
> The people I ran around with went to college bars
> And drank beer and talked about getting laid
> And made jokes about girls and talked about their parents
> And talked about what they were going to do to succeed.
> The tough guys never talk about that shit.
> The attitude you know. It's against the rules.[14]

According to the story, Ashley and his friend went toward Detroit late one night to get a snack, and afterward, driving in his friend's custom-modified ("two-door, chopped and channeled") car and discussing theosophy, his friend accidentally bumped, slightly, the car in front of them. (To chop a car is to lower the roof by cutting down the pillars and windows to create less wind resistance and more appearance for speed; to channel it is to remove the floor and refasten it higher inside the body, thus bringing the car closer to the ground. Ashley's continuing love of cars stems from his Detroit background.) The car in front backed up and bumped them back, harder, and Ashley's friend reciprocated, pushing the front car into the intersection. The four men in the front car, suburbanites, they speculate, got out looking for a fight, and Ashley braced for being beaten up.

> My friend says, "Don't get out, it's not worth it."
> He means it's not up to par as far as fun goes.
> He just backs up another ten feet
> And puts it to the floor with the clutch in.
> There's a huge roar in the car.
> He says, "Let 'em all get out and we can hit 'em all at once."
> At this point the suburbanites come to their senses . . .
> They drive away as fast as they can.
> My friend follows them for a couple of blocks
> About one foot between the cars.
> As fast as they can go.
> The suburbanites are really speeding,
> But the car is shit and the guy can't drive anyway.

Also he's scared.
I'm not scared anymore, strangely.
After a couple of blocks my friend turns off and we keep cruising,
Talking about Theosophy.[15]

Another story tells of Ashley and two friends getting beaten up by two tough gay men they had accidentally run across who were making love in a public park. We also learn in *Celestial Excursions* that, after his father's death, the neighbor's house blew up due to a gas leak caused by a tornado, setting the Brookwood house on fire.

Ashley says that his parents never discouraged his musical aspirations. "Their idea of money is that you get paid on Friday afternoon," he says, "so if you get paid on Friday afternoon, what does it matter what you do?" The University High School lacked any kind of music program, however; the school counselor told him he shouldn't want to be a musician and promised to get him a scholarship at some engineering school. Ashley replied, "But I don't want to be an engineer, I want to be a musician," and since the counselor wouldn't recommend him for a music program, Ashley himself wrote the University of Michigan music department a letter, which was never answered. As Ashley recalled in an interview, he got into the university almost by accident.

> It must have been about August in my 18th year, and I decided to just go on the road. So I started hitchhiking around, and I wound up in St. Louis without any money, which is sort of embarrassing. But I knew a girl, she was the girlfriend of one of my high school friends, whose family lived in either Louisville or Lexington, I can't remember, and I knew that they had money. She was a real good friend of mine, and I knew that if I could get to where she lived, she would lend me the money to get to California, 50 bucks, you know. So I hitchhiked to Louisville, or wherever it was. I mean, I didn't have any money. Her family wasn't too happy to see me, they put me in a cheesy hotel downtown. And she came down the next morning in her convertible, and she said, "Your mom called last night and the University of Michigan's music department said if you wanted to get in you could come and audition on Monday morning." This was on Thursday. I said, "Can you lend me some money to get home?" She said, "Sure." She gave me the money. So I took the bus home, and I practiced my whatever it was, Mozart, or something. But I didn't say I wanted to be a piano major, that would have been foolish. I just said I wanted to be a theory major, which covered everything, and so they let me in.

Ashley attended the University of Michigan from 1948 to 1952. As he puts it, "I loved having people who were real smart telling me things that I could otherwise never know." (This was quite a contrast to his sister Anne Ward, who was accepted by Northwestern University in Chicago, was driven there by their mother, looked at her dorm, and said, "I don't want to go to college. This is crazy. Who would do this?" They turned around and went home.)

The dean of the music school at Michigan in the 1950s was the formidable Earl V. Moore, who, along with Howard Hanson at the University of Rochester's Eastman School of Music, "did more to shape baccalaureate music degree programs as they developed in the United States than any other person."[16] During Moore's tenure the music department underwent rapid expansion. The catalogue for 1944–45 lists forty-five music faculty members; by 1952–53 that number had swelled to seventy-one, not counting nonresident lecturers and teaching fellows. The Eastman-educated Homer Keller (1915–96), a composer of robustly rhythmic tonal music, was teaching at Michigan when Ashley arrived. Ashley took his theory classes and found him "light-hearted" and funny. In 1949 the more famous Ross Lee Finney (1906–97) joined the faculty. He had studied with the celebrated French composition teacher Nadia Boulanger, with the conservative Edward Burlingame Hill at Harvard University, with Alban Berg in Vienna in 1931–32, and with the august 12-tone composer Roger Sessions (1896–1985). Because of his wide European experience, Finney had been welcomed during World War II into the Office of Strategic Services as a civilian captain and had worked at making maps and locating potential targets in France; once he was slightly wounded by a land mine.[17] This gave him a rather dashing reputation at the university. "Everyone treated him as if he [were] James Bond," Ashley says.

A folk music enthusiast and performer, Finney had gone through an "Americana" phase, often quoting American tunes in his music. In the aftermath of war, however, the charms of musical patriotism began to pall, and he turned toward 12-tone technique at about the time he came to Michigan; his String Quartet no. 6 of 1950, though officially in the key of E, was his first work to use tone rows.[18] By the late 1950s he was applying serial techniques to elements other than pitch, keeping up with the advances being pioneered in Europe by Pierre Boulez and Karlheinz Stockhausen. In addition to classes and private teaching, Finney offered weekly analysis seminars that ushered students through works by Bach, Bartók, Hindemith, and others.[19] As a participant in these, Ashley wrote a paper on a Bartók string quartet that, he recalls, met with Finney's approval. Ashley would also become a graduate student of Leslie Bassett (b. 1923), a Finney student who joined the faculty in 1952. As evinced by his Trio for Clarinet, Viola, and Piano (1953), Bassett was, at the time, writing music that pushed the boundaries of tonality in a lyrical manner.

The professor whom Ashley remembers with the most affection was the important Bach scholar Hans T. David (1902–67), who was appointed to the faculty in 1950.[20] Born in Bavaria, David had become one of the world's leading Bach experts by the time his doctorate was conferred in 1928. Leaving Germany soon after the advent of the Nazis, he relocated to the United States in the 1930s and became the editor of the impressive *Bach Reader*, published in 1946. His particular passion was for intricate canons, strict contrapuntal devices, and musical puzzles; one can easily imagine this early influence leading to Ashley's eventual respect for and interest in strict composing formulas. Ashley took David's harmony class, taught at 8:00 in the morning, and also attended his once-a-week seminars on the "more sophisticated" aspects of Bach. "He had the idea that J. S. was absolutely symmetrical; everything that happened at the beginning happened at the end of the piece," Ashley recalls. David was described by the co-editor of the *Bach Reader*, Arthur Mendel, as possessing "a personal warmth and childlike sweetness."[21]

Ashley also studied with an assistant professor of piano, Mary S. Fishburne, who had gotten her master's at Michigan and had done graduate work at the New England Conservatory of Music and at Harvard.[22] Ashley credits her with exercising considerable influence over him. One summer she ran into him as he was delivering ice. When school resumed, she told him that delivering ice was an unacceptable job for a musician. Ashley remonstrated, "But that's the best-paying job I can get." She said, "You can't deliver ice and be a musician. You have to get a different kind of job." For the remaining summers of his undergrad years, Ashley delivered mail, relieving local postmen when they went on vacation; doubtless his father's connections proved helpful. Assistant Professor Fishburne, M. Mus., was listed in the school catalogue only from 1949 to 1956, and from there vanished from history.

The University of Michigan music program at the time was a preordained curriculum with no electives until the junior year. As a theory major, Ashley would have had to study two instruments, music literature, English, history, German, composition in his junior year, and more advanced theory courses such as orchestration and keyboard harmony. (Had he majored in composition, the only difference would have been composition lessons in his first two years in lieu of the second instrument.) Even aside from Hans David, the department was heavily Bach-oriented. The first-year Basic Musicianship course was defined as "analysis of Bach as found in the chorale harmonizations," continuing "through a survey of the styles of Haydn, Mozart, and Beethoven." Ashley remembers his English courses with particular enthusiasm because they introduced him to James Joyce and T. S. Eliot; in the opera *Concrete* he would represent himself carrying around a James Joyce book in the army "like a bible." In 1951, H. Wiley Hitchcock (1923–2007), who would become his generation's foremost musicologist of American music, joined the music literature faculty as an instructor.

Upon graduating in 1952, Ashley wanted to get out of Ann Arbor. He moved to New York City and enrolled as a piano and composition major in the Manhattan School of Music, which, as a trade school, one could attend simply by paying the $240 tuition for a semester. Ashley, as he puts it, was never good at getting recommendations and didn't have any. At first he studied briefly with Ursula Mamlok (b. 1923), a Berlin-born composer whose early style stemmed from Paul Hindemith's and who was later drawn to 12-tone technique; she was a graduate student at the time. Then the faculty composer Vittorio Giannini (1903–66), a conservative writer of Italianate operas, took a sabbatical, and the more radical but nonetheless distinguished Wallingford Riegger (1885–1961) was hired as a replacement. He was Ashley's first sympathetic and influential composition teacher.

Born in Georgia, Riegger had studied at the Berlin Hochschule für Musik and was forced to return to the United States by the events of World War I. Failing at a career as a conductor, he turned seriously to composing in the 1920s and in 1927 produced a groundbreaking and at first highly controversial work for strings, *Study in Sonority*, which followed and even anticipated the most radical trends coming out of Arnold Schoenberg's work in Vienna. In the 1930s he settled into his own version of 12-tone style, using Schoenberg's 12-tone technique in his own less doctrinaire way in his third and fourth symphonies and his Concerto for Piano and Woodwind Quintet. A communist, he was called to testify before the House Un-American Activities Committee in 1957.[23] Along with the composers Charles Ives, Carl Ruggles, Henry Cowell, and John Becker, he is considered one of the "American Five," the first generation of major American composers working in indigenous styles, though his methods drew more from European aesthetics than did the others'.

What delighted Ashley was that the Manhattan School of Music was on the Upper East Side at 105th Street; he and Riegger both had apartments at about that latitude on the Upper West Side, so they would ride the bus to school together and talk politics. Though worried about potential persecution for his radical connections during the Red Scare of the 1950s, Riegger, Ashley says, "gave me quite a few lectures on the evils of our system, which I took to heart. I agreed with him entirely." More to the point, Riegger was teaching 12-tone technique, which most of the students found off-putting; Ashley loved it. Some time after graduating he received a card from Riegger saying something like (as best he could remember), "The road you've picked has very many difficulties, but never give up." Ashley was touched; he refers to the note as a "laying on of hands."

Ashley describes a meaningful epiphany he had during his graduate school period with a recording of the Berg Chamber Concerto:

I listened to that at least once a week and sometimes much more often for at least a year. I never could understand what was happening. Then I came to New York, one Saturday morning, a beautiful morning, and I came back up to my room and put that record on, and I understood it *totally*. I *understood* what Berg was doing. I must have listened to it fifty times without understanding. I didn't *gradually* learn it, I learned it in however long it took to play it that Saturday morning. I loved Alban Berg. I played his sonata pretty well. I like Schoenberg; I like his ideas. I didn't like his music, it was too rhythmically . . . too *predictable* in some weird kind of way. [But later,] when I started to hear real people's music, friends of mine, that was all I wanted to do.

Ashley's Manhattan apartment was in the International House at 122 Street and Claremont Avenue, across from the old Juilliard School of Music. Another apartment on the same floor was occupied by a painter named George Manupelli (b. 1931), who would become an experimental filmmaker and an important influence in Ashley's life. Manupelli was drafted into the army in 1953 but returned frequently to New York to see his Boston-based girlfriend Betty Johnson, who introduced Ashley to her art student friend Mary Tsaltas (ca. 1931–96), a Boston girl who was training at the Massachusetts College of Art. (A first-generation Greek American, she was never certain about her birth date.) According to Manupelli, Ashley and Mary decided to get married after about thirty hours together, though Ashley says it was three weeks. In any case, on April 11, 1954, the two couples were married in a joint ceremony, with the brides in leotards and skirts. As Betty Johnson recalled years later, "Mary and I got on the midnight bus to New York, married Bob and George, went back to Boston, and were in art school on Monday."[24]

Ashley himself was getting letters from the draft board—and ignoring them. Graduating with his master's degree without a job in 1954, he went with Mary to Puerto Rico to join Manupelli, who was stationed in the army there. The lure of the island at the time was that Puerto Ricans who joined the army could train on the island rather than be shipped elsewhere; also, the Puerto Rican camps were rumored to be slack about discipline. Manupelli was due to be discharged soon, and as a desk worker in the general's office, he thought he could turn his job over to Ashley. By late 1954 Mary was pregnant. Though still reluctant to enter the army ("The idea of getting bossed around was always hard for me to take"), Ashley couldn't find a job, didn't speak Spanish, and was desperate for money. A doctor warned that the baby was likely to be born prematurely. Ashley telegrammed the draft board, saying he was sorry he hadn't responded, but he'd been traveling. The draft board telegrammed back, instructing him to hie himself to the nearest

Army Recruitment Center the coming Friday morning. On Monday Ashley was sworn into the army, and a few days later, on February 9, 1955, Mary gave birth to their son Sam, who was several weeks premature. Mother and son received good care in the army hospital, and Ashley thanks his lucky stars that he got into the army in time for the birth.

The practice of training those to be stationed in Puerto Rico locally, however, came to a precipitous end. Ashley was stationed at Fort Dix, New Jersey, for basic training. ("I learned how to shoot a gun. It's all silliness.") In April or May he was transferred to Fort Hood, near Killeen, Texas, between Waco and Austin. He found a shack to put Mary and Sam in, and for the next eighteen months sat out the waning Korean War playing clarinet and bassoon in the concert band, cymbals in the marching band, and piano in the jazz band, as well as in several small local combos in his spare time.[25] Though the army-issue instruments were terrible, and he insists he was a terrible player on all the instruments, Ashley enjoyed the work immensely.

One of the stories in *Dust* is a tale of the Fort Hood days. Ashley often worked nights, playing in bands to make a little more money. While Mary and Sam were at home, a couple of men would come by, sit in the car with the motor running, and whisper menacingly to Mary, trying to get her to come out. She'd pretend no one was home, but it got to be terrifying. Ashley called the police, who only advised him to buy a gun and shoot the men when they came around: "It'll never even come to court. / Happens all the time. / Texas."[26] Ashley consulted with a gun-owning friend who brought over a huge pistol, but Ashley and Mary hated even to look at it, secreted it in a kitchen drawer, and then got so they couldn't stand to open the drawer. So they went to a pawn shop and bought a little gun with pearl on the handle. The gun-owning friend laughed his head off when he saw it. Finally the men came by while Ashley was in the house, and as he ran out with the gun, they were speeding off. He hid, waiting for them, but they never came back. He threw the gun away.

Upon his release from the army in 1956, Ashley headed with his wife and child back to Ann Arbor to seek a doctorate at the University of Michigan, which, as a state resident, he could attend more cheaply than any other school. He now had a family to support, and given his small miscellany of marketable skills, teaching seemed like the only secure career. This time he was determined to get his degree in composition rather than in theory, but his plans hit a formidable obstacle in the person of Finney. Ashley's music did not impress the man. Ashley brought Finney a piece he had written while in the army. Finney gave his response: "Nobody can play this." Ashley responded, "Of course they can. I *know*. You give me the cello and I'll play it." But Finney remained intransigent. After dropping out of school briefly, Ashley went back and studied composition with Leslie Bassett instead. Nevertheless, Ashley recalls, every time he brought a composition to the faculty, Finney would pronounce it unplayable. Nor was Ashley the only student so received. When Ashley's future ONCE festival colleague Gordon Mumma (b. 1935) entered the school as a composition major, Finney took a look at his first piece, crumpled it up, and threw it out the window. Disgusted, Mumma switched to the literature department.[27]

"Ross Finney and I didn't get along at all," Ashley says. "I always thought that Finney was a bitter man and that he had some grievance against the celebrity of Aaron Copland, or somebody like that. He was stuck out in Ann Arbor, and Copland was writing for Broadway. He didn't like me, and I didn't like him." Such a view of Finney is not uncommon, though Ashley's fellow student and future ONCE festival cohort Roger Reynolds (b. 1934) was a touch more sympathetic: "He could be imperious, though you knew in your heart that what he said was true."[28] Finney would later admit, "If I was sometimes very harsh in my advice to students, it was because I dreaded giving too much encouragement to those who lacked talent or commitment." Nevertheless, looking back in his 1992 autobiography, Finney singled out Ashley and Reynolds as two students of his who "made their mark as American composers."[29]

As so often happens, the detour Ashley had to take around speed-bump Finney turned out to be a blessing in disguise. The university had a Speech Research Institute funded by Bell Laboratories whose director, Gordon Peterson, took an interest in Ashley. "I started studying at the speech lab," Ashley says, "because they had equipment, they had tape recorders. It wasn't Stockhausen's studio, but it was a studio." The Speech Research Institute was attempting to replicate speech artificially, something that would become commonplace by the 1980s but was a difficult nut to crack in the early days of computer audio. For three years from 1957 to 1960, Ashley did doctoral work on the causes of stuttering, taking courses in speech, linguistics, and logic. He aided a doctoral student who was doing work on the microsecond delay that interrupts the circuit between the brain and the issuance of the intended word.[30] More important, though, he learned to work with electronic sound equipment, particularly in its application to the human voice. The technological expertise gained there would serve Ashley well his entire life, especially during the 1960s, and would eventually land him a job at Mills College.

Ashley's mentor was hired by the University of Pittsburgh to set up another research studio, and he offered to let Ashley take over his project. Within months, Ashley could have had a doctorate in psychoacoustics. "I was right on the edge," he says, "of being a scientist. Because I thought, at least I can support my family. All I had to do was say yes, and I couldn't do it. I went into [Peterson's] office and said, 'I appreciate very much everything you've done for me, but I promised myself I was going to be a composer, and I think I should keep that promise.' He stuck his hand across the desk and said, 'Good choice.'"

In 1958 Ashley suffered an emotional trauma. As a result of taking medicine for an inner-ear infection, he suffered terribly from tinnitus, or ringing in the ears, and saw an ear doctor about it. The doctor prescribed a series of painful weekly scrapings of the eardrum that would continue for months. Finally he gave Ashley the bad news that he would go deaf in seven years. It must have been a particularly fateful blow for a man who'd grown up with a deaf father, and Ashley was especially incensed by the biblical connotations of the projected time frame. A few months later he decided that the doctor was just wrong, as, indeed, turned out to be the case. The story is recounted in the libretto to one of his most closely autobiographical operas, *Foreign Experiences*.

By 1957 the connections that would lead to the ONCE festivals were multiplying thick and fast; Ann Arbor was a talent magnet. As a literature major, Gordon Mumma started composing music for the department's theatrical productions, learning how to manipulate taped sound on the department's reel-to-reel player. While hanging around the College of Architecture and Design, Mumma met Milton Cohen (1924–95), a professor of art who was developing a high-tech light show called the Space Theater.[31] Cohen was working with Harold Borkin (b. 1934), an electronics genius who graduated from the College of Architecture and Design in 1957. Along with fellow graduate Joseph Wehrer (b. 1926), they built a fifty-foot-wide, twenty-sided icosahedral dome of triangular canvas panels held together with aluminum tubes and placed within it an irregular "tree of mirrors." In the center of the room were slide and movie projectors, overhead projectors, filters, prisms, and other light sources capable of producing a dizzying kaleidoscope of colors and abstract or photographic images.[32] Cohen wanted electronic music to accompany the show, so he enlisted Mumma, who brought Ashley on board as co-composer.

In 1959 Ashley got his first real break from the University of Michigan music department. Finney was awarded the Prix de Rome and would spend the year abroad. Meanwhile, his replacement would turn out to be a boon for Ashley. During the war, Finney had met the Catalan composer Roberto Gerhard (1896–1970), who had been exiled from his native Spain by the Spanish Civil War; Barcelona had fallen while he was in France, and it was unsafe to return. Finney wrote to Gerhard and offered him his position for the year as well as his house to live in.[33] Gerhard would become Ashley's second sympathetic composition teacher and a close friend.

A student of the Spanish nationalist composer Enrique Granados, Gerhard was working in parallel with Stravinsky and Bartók in the appropriation of folk materials—Spanish, in his case—into symphonic music. In Spain Gerhard had been a major promoter of Schoenberg's music. As music professor at the Escola Normal de la Generalitat in Barcelona, he had been a major force behind the 1936 International Society for Contemporary Music festival, at which Alban Berg's Violin Concerto had received its premiere. In June 1939 he accepted a one-year position at King's College in Cambridge. He remained in England and became a British citizen in 1960,[34] but in England his Spanish nationalist style had less urgency and met with little comprehension. Exile, however, would bring a new direction to Gerhard's efforts. During the 1940s Gerhard relied mostly on freelance composing for film and theater, but he also increased the application of Schoenbergian row technique in his music. "A composer," Gerhard wrote, "needs grace (inspiration), guts, intellect, madness; and systems are a *sine qua non*, because the intellect can only work, only take grip, when confronted by a system."[35] Nevertheless, he was dubious about music that appealed more to the intellect than to the ear, and his large works of the 1950s and 1960s are more notable for their timbral colors and unusual textures than for any audible strict use of tone rows. Moreover, it was a sign of Gerhard's openness to radical ideas that he was the first major composer in Britain to work in the new electronic medium. From 1954 to 1959 he completed ten electronic pieces, some with live ensemble, the tapes made on two reel-to-reel players at his home studio;[36] he referred to his *musique concrète* as "sound composition." He eventually received assistance at the BBC Radiophonic Workshop.

Invited to America for the first time in 1960, Gerhard deeply involved himself in the Ann Arbor music scene and became a father figure and catalyst to the younger composers. Unbeknownst to them, he suffered from a heart condition that would eventually kill him, and his wife Leopoldina protected him from overexertion. A photograph taken in 1960 shows him in the yard of Leslie Bassett's house, surrounded by Bassett, Reynolds, Ashley, George Cacioppo, and other aspiring composers. Ashley and Gerhard became good friends, and the older man paid the supreme compliment to Ashley's music up to that point: For Cohen's Space Theater, Ashley had made a violent-sounding electronic piece using metal dowels with weights screwed onto the ends so that they could be plucked and would vibrate against a table and that could be moved to change the pitch; "really noisy," Ashley says. Gerhard, meanwhile, had received a commission from the

Koussevitsky Foundation for an orchestral work that would be titled *Collages* (in 1967 he would retitle the piece Symphony no. 3, with the subtitle *Collages*). It was his first work for orchestra and electronic tape, the most ambitious work yet for that medium aside from Edgard Varèse's 1954 *Deserts.* Gerhard was impressed by Ashley's dowel piece and asked him if he could use it as part of the tape component of his orchestral piece. "I said, 'Are you kidding?'" Ashley recalls. "I was so flattered I didn't know what to do." Listening to Gerhard's symphony for the first time in 2009, however, Ashley couldn't locate his music in the tape part and thought that Gerhard ended up not using it after all.

By 1960 Ann Arbor was a hotbed of cutting-edge musical activity. The German giant Karlheinz Stockhausen (1928–2007), less than two years older than Ashley but already famous in Europe, came to lecture at the University of Michigan in 1958 and exhorted the students to take the presenting of their music into their own hands.[37] Roger Reynolds had finished an engineering degree at Michigan in 1957 and a year later returned from California to start graduate work in music. Reynolds had met John Cage in New York, and he invited Cage and the pianist David Tudor to lecture and perform in Ann Arbor on May 14 and 16, 1960, the visit sponsored by the College of Architecture and Design and the Dramatic Arts Center.[38] One of these performances was a piece called *Indeterminacy*, in which Cage simply told one story per minute while Tudor independently played electronic noises; the importance of this storytelling-over-noise-background paradigm for Ashley's operas may be worth emphasizing. That same month, Ashley convinced a local electronics genius, Uolevi Lahti, to sponsor an appearance by Luciano Berio at his record store, where Berio played his 1958 tape piece *Omaggio a Joyce*. Meanwhile, in 1957 Ashley's old friend Manupelli, now a filmmaker, had started a job at Central Michigan University.[39] In 1958 Manupelli made a film called *The Image in Time*, for which Ashley created what is apparently the first electroacoustic soundtrack in film history.[40]

Then, from August 7 to 14, 1960, Ashley, Reynolds, Mumma, and George Cacioppo (1926–84) drove to Stratford, Ontario, for an international composers' conference presented by the Canadian League of Composers and featuring Berio, Varèse, Roy Harris, Ernst Krenek, George Rochberg, Henri Dutilleux, and others. Though excited by the music, the four young composers were frustrated that the festival discouraged contact with the "great men." On the way home, Ashley said, "We could do a better festival than that," and by the time they got out of the car, the first ONCE Festival was planned. Ashley had no reason to know it yet, but he was in the right place at the right time and was about to plunge into the very center of the American (and European) avant-garde for the next ten years.

3 When Slow Starts to Mean Something, We Crave Fast

The ONCE Years

WHAT ASHLEY REFERS TO AS "the glorious chaos of the 1960's"[1] started for him years before it hit the culture at large. Before the Beatles became famous, before the Vietnam protests, before "flower power" and love-ins and men with long hair, the young composers of Ann Arbor launched boldly into a provocative new era. From the outset, the music of the ONCE festivals seemed new and crazy; as one critic wrote at the time, "ONCE isn't music as the term is usually used, and it isn't entertainment as the term is usually used. Last night's concert was a great auditory purgative—a weird fun world of its own."[2] Forty-five years later, recordings of that music still sound pretty bizarre. There's often an insouciant aimlessness to the music that can make it seem like the haphazard or unintended result of an inscrutable process, which sometimes is exactly the case. Still, if out in left field, the ONCE composers weren't working in a vacuum; as Ashley says, "There was a point around 1965 when I knew every composer in America and Europe, and knew what they were doing."[3] They may have been relatively extreme, but Ashley and his friends were a conscious and well-informed part of an international avant-garde.

The two major musical movements in play at the time seem so contradictory as to belong to different worlds. One was serialism. Starting in 1921, the Austrian composer Arnold Schoenberg had begun a new method of composing by drawing every melody and harmony in a piece from a specific ordering of the 12 pitches in an octave, a 12-tone row or series. After World War II, the 12-tone method seemed to offer a chance to create a new musical world from scratch, free from the taint of Romanticist tropes whose nationalist associations had come to seem suspect. Composers like Stockhausen and Pierre Boulez (b. 1925) in Europe and Milton Babbitt (1916–2011) in America started expanding the row concept into the fields of rhythm, timbre, and dynamics. These came to be called the "parameters" of music, and by structuring them independently via precompositional numerical schemes, one could create a complex musical object that seemed to possess a kind of scientific objectivity. To this day, with his fanatically predetermined operatic structures in mind, Ashley half-ironically refers to himself as a serialist.[4]

The other movement was conceptualism. In 1952 John Cage (1912–92) had premiered a piece called *4′33″* in which David Tudor sat at a piano silently for four and a half minutes. Accepting the parametric definitions of his European counterparts, Cage began using chance methods to compose his music. Suddenly, the theoretical gulf between scientific determinism and randomness seemed to shrink into insignificance; often the listener couldn't tell which was which. Freed by *4′33″* to consider all (and no) sounds music, and to replace the 12-tone row with any algorithm or process that came to mind, imaginations ran wild. Cage's students at the New School for Social Research in New York became part of a conceptualist movement called Fluxus in which various actions were prescribed rather than notated. La Monte Young (b. 1935) directed the performer to feed a piano hay. Annea Lockwood (b. 1939 in New Zealand) burned pianos amplified with asbestos-covered microphones. In *Homage to John Cage*, Korean-born Nam June Paik (1932–2006) cut off Cage's tie, poured shaving cream on his head, left the hall, and telephoned from down the street to say the piece was over.[5] Another of his pieces directed the performer to "creep into the vagina of a living whale."[6] Boundaries between music, literature, theater, visual art, and film became indistinct; poets worked with sound, composers made graphics, visual artists made theater.

The conceptualist pursuits of Young, Terry Riley (b. 1935), and Steve Reich (b. 1936) led to playing around with tape loops, and their delight with the pleasures of repetition led to yet another new wrinkle called minimalism. Early minimalist music was made up of drones or repeating musical figures often put through gradual transformations so slow as to be barely perceptible. Similarly, Cage's associate Morton Feldman (1926–87) invented a new, floating continuity for music in which motives and sonorities could appear and reappear in musical landscapes extending eventually to four, five, or six hours.

The ONCE festival represented a kind of crunching together of serialism and conceptualism with a characteristically Midwestern disregard for consistency or ideology. Pieces based on intricate systems were common, as were pieces based on verbal instructions, the two techniques cross-fading into each other. Within the conceptualist milieu, one distinctive thing about Ashley was that he seemed less interested in sonic patterns than in the social situation of the performance. After Cage, Ashley wrote in 1961, the guiding metaphor of music was no longer sound but time, and the ultimate result might be "a music that wouldn't necessarily involve anything but the presence of people. . . . It seems to me that the most radical redefinition of music that I could think of would be one that defines 'music' without reference to sound."[7] At the same time, however, Ashley also shared with the minimalists a new passion for music that abandoned traditional rhetoric, that eschewed sections and climaxes, that simulated and evoked an eternal present. Later in life, he would redefine the '60s moment in an almost opposite way that suggested affinities with Morton Feldman and the minimalists:

> The only thing that's interesting to me right now is that, up to me and a couple of other guys, music had always been about eventfulness: like, when things happened, and if they happened, whether they would be a surprise, or an enjoyment, or something like that . . . It's about eventfulness. And I was never interested in eventfulness. I was only interested in sound. I mean, just literally, sound in the Morton Feldman sense. . . . There's a quality in music that is outside of time, that is not related to time. And that has always fascinated me. . . . That's sort of what I'm all about, from the first until the most recent. A lot of people are back into eventfulness. But it's very boring. Eventfulness is really boring.

The earliest piece of concert music acknowledged on Ashley's list of works is the 1959 Piano Sonata, which later acquired the breathtaking subtitle *Christopher Columbus Crosses to the New World in the Niña, the Pinta, and the Santa Maria Using Only Dead Reckoning and a Crude Astrolabe*. The title alludes to the fact that there are three movements as alike as the ships with which Columbus sailed to the New World, two of them shadows of the other, in the usual "schoolbook image."[8] In 1959, however, only the first movement was completed, the inspiration for the other two not arriving until twenty years later, when "Blue" Gene Tyranny asked to be allowed to record the work. In extended serialist fashion, the sonata is based on a series of thirty-six pitches and a schedule of pitch events. Dense, dissonant, virtuosic, and nonlinear, it inhabits a style continuous with Stockhausen's *Klavierstücke* of the 1950s. Ashley himself premiered it at the University of Michigan's Angell Hall on March 6, 1960,[9] giving us a sense that he was a very good pianist at the time. It was the last work he would compose in conventional musical notation for thirty-two years, until the far more serene *Van Cao's Meditation* for piano (1992) appeared. The sonata is not recognizably related to any of Ashley's mature music, yet he was proud enough of it to issue it on one of the first recordings on Mimi Johnson's Lovely Music label in 1979.

Scenes (for example, Vienna in the 1780s, Paris in the 1920s, New York in the 1970s) are extremely lucky, unpredictable, unexplainable occurrences in the history of the arts, and the ONCE festival—apparently so named because of predictions it would only happen once[10]—created an impressive scene, indeed. Crucial to its existence was Anne Wehrer (1929–2007, née Counselman), a woman of phenomenal energy and persuasiveness, the patron saint of the ONCE festivals and wife of architecture professor Joseph Wehrer. At eighteen she had lost a leg to bone cancer, but she adjusted to her prosthesis so well that the fact rarely comes up in descriptions of her.[11] She was a member of the board of Ann Arbor's Dramatic Arts Center, which had been founded in the 1950s to bring in experimental theater groups from New York City. Also on the board was Wilfrid Kaplan (b. 1915), a mathematics professor who had become fairly wealthy because of royalties from a widely used calculus textbook he had written.[12] Kaplan would become the financial force behind the ONCE festivals. On October 16, 1960, Ashley and Reynolds went with Anne Wehrer to the Dramatic Arts Committee, and Kaplan agreed to provide the funding.

The first ONCE concerts were performed at the First Unitarian Church in Ann Arbor on February 24 and 25, and March 3 and 4, 1961. The initial two concerts, featuring Luciano Berio and the pianist Paul Jacobs, were largely devoted to recent European music by Berio, Krenek, Stockhausen, Olivier Messiaen, Anton Webern, Sylvano Bussotti, Roman Haubenstock-Ramati, and others. The second pair of concerts featured music by the festival's organizers—Ashley, Cacioppo, Mumma, Reynolds, Donald Scavarda—and two University of Michigan graduate composers, Bruce Wise and Van Solkema. Ashley played his sonata, along with pieces by Mumma, Scavarda, and Reynolds, and presented his tape piece *The Fourth of July* and George Manupelli's film *The Bottleman* with Ashley's soundtrack. According to Leta Miller's admirably thorough documentation of the ONCE years, costs came to $1,300; ticket sales from the standing-room-only crowds brought in more than expected, $1,175.[13] The festival was immediately a resounding success. Further concerts were ultimately scheduled as follows:

1962: 6 concerts, February 9–11, 16–18
1963: 4 concerts, February 9–10, 16–17
1964: 7 concerts, February 25–29, March 1

1965: 4 concerts, February 11–14
3 concerts, September 17–19
1966: 2 recording concerts, March 28, 29
1968: 3 concerts, February 8–10
1969: *The Trial of Anne Opie Wehrer*, January 31, February 1

As Richard S. James documented, the nature of the ONCE festivals changed in the middle of 1964. In the first two and a half years, the event was run as a contemporary music festival, at first dominated by performances of European scores, gradually becoming more and more centered on local composers. In 1964, however, the events started becoming more theatrical, more imbued with dance, sculpture, public theater, and elements that would later lead to the genre dubbed performance art.[14] Part of this change came from Mary Ashley's activities. Starting in May 1963, she staged an annual event, theatrical in premise but with a sculptural aesthetic, called "Truck: Unscheduled Private Events in the Midst of an Unsuspecting Public Audience." The first of these events was also to be the most disruptive: as an audience emerged from a local orchestra concert, they were greeted by performers in a number of parked cars. Ashley was draped over the seat of a Pontiac as though dead; a pianist played an upright piano in a van; a woman protruded from the sun roof of a vehicle putting curlers in her hair; other members passed out peanut butter and jelly sandwiches. Although the group had obtained permission in advance from the city, traffic congestion became a problem, and the police became mildly involved. Mary's performers called themselves the Truck (ensemble), which quickly evolved into the ONCE Group. Its original members were the Ashleys, the Mummas, the Wehrers, the Borkins, and Caroline Cohen. From 1964 to 1969 they performed several of Ashley's most ambitious works, including *That Morning Thing*, *Kittyhawk*, *Joy Road Interchange* (later called *The Lecture Series* on tour), and *The Trial of Anne Opie Wehrer*.

One of Ashley's most important future collaborators arrived in Ann Arbor in time for the ONCE festival's second year: Robert Sheff, a phenomenal pianist and composer who would later take the stage name "Blue" Gene Tyranny. Born in San Antonio in 1945, Tyranny and his high school chum Philip Krumm (b. 1941) put on concerts of avant-garde music in their home town. Tyranny, a pianist who could sight-read virtually anything and perform and improvise brilliantly in any style, impressed a visiting Juilliard faculty member so much that he was invited to apply to Juilliard. Accepted, he visited New York City and realized that not only would the school require him to take courses in subjects he'd already mastered but that his graphic and Cage-inspired scores wouldn't meet with approval from the conservative faculty. Meanwhile, Krumm had already visited Ann Arbor and told Tyranny, "They're doing things here like we did in San Antonio," so Tyranny bade New York a hasty goodbye and took a bus to Ann Arbor. As he says of ONCE today, "It wasn't just a once-a-year festival, it was a lifestyle. Everybody in town was involved in it one way or another; every aspect of the sixties was involved with it."[15]

One regular in the ONCE festival audiences was an eccentric local boy named Jim Osterberg (b. 1947), who, because he played in a rock band called the Iguanas, acquired the nickname Iggy; he would go on to punk rock fame as leader of the innovative band Iggy Pop and the Stooges. Tyranny toured with the group as its pianist in the 1970s, and sometime later Ashley even talked to Pop about the possibility of his performing in Ashley's ensemble. That didn't happen, but Pop's autobiography *I Need More* was co-written with Anne Wehrer. Meanwhile, Tyranny would go on to play piano in most of Ashley's operas, and for some of them he created a large part of the characterization of their musical surface.

In 1964 the Italian composer Luigi Nono (who would become a good friend of Ashley's) arranged an invitation for Milton Cohen's Space Theater to perform at the Venice Biennale; this would be Ashley's first trip to Europe. In another spin-off from the ONCE activities, Ashley and Mumma toured from 1962 to 1967, giving a series of concerts called "Music for Pianos," playing mostly on Midwest college campuses and radio stations but also performing in London in 1966 and in Athens, Rome, and Brussels in 1967.[16]

From 1966 to 1977 Ashley toured with Mumma and the composers Alvin Lucier (b. 1931) and David Behrman as the Sonic Arts Union. Lucier, a New Hampshire native, had emerged from Yale University as a composer of neoclassical music, and in 1963 he took a job directing the choral union at Brandeis University. Contact with Cage, however, turned him in a more experimental direction, and he began working with acoustic phenomena such as resonances of rooms and containers and beats between slightly out-of-tune pitches. Lucier's best-known work is *I Am Sitting in a Room* (1970), in which he records his voice in a room, plays the recording and records that, plays that recording and records it, and so on, as successive recordings increasingly trigger and amplify the resonant frequencies of the room until his obscured voice is transformed into a hollow roar. (In 1970 Lucier took a position in electronic music at Wesleyan University.) Behrman (born to American parents in Salzburg in 1937) attended Harvard, where he gave concerts with Frederic Rzewski and Christian Wolff, and Columbia University. During the late 1960s he served as producer of the important "Music of Our Time" series for Columbia Masterworks recordings. Meeting Mumma in 1964 sparked his interest in making music with electronic circuitry, and his subsequent works have often taken the form of software environments with which live acoustic performers interact.

Ashley invited Lucier and Behrman to perform at the ONCE festival, and Lucier, in turn, brought Ashley, Mumma, and Behrman to Brandeis. As Ashley tells it, after the latter concert they were enjoying drinks at Lucier's house, and Ashley said, "Alvin, look. Every time someone writes you a letter, and asks you to give a concert, and then there's that tender moment when they're not sure whether you're worth it, you say, I'll give you a concert and it also has Robert Ashley, Gordon Mumma, and David Behrman. Then you'll be sure to get the concert. He said, that's a good idea, let's do that. David and Gordon were in the other room doing something, and we brought 'em in and said, how about this for an idea? And they all said, yeah."

The four toured together for eleven years. They never actually performed together; each person would play his own music, and the others were available to turn knobs, adjust the electronics, and help with logistics. Aside from playing at American schools all over the East and West Coasts, they toured cities in Europe from Stockholm to Zagreb in April and May 1969 and had another European tour two years later, plus a 1974 performance at Festival d'Automne in Paris, where Ashley would first work with Joan La Barbara. Just as significant, the Sonic Arts Union released a vinyl record in 1971 on the Mainstream label that introduced their music, and the whole genre of interactive electronic music, to a wider audience. The disc contained *Purposeful Lady Slow Afternoon*, Mumma's *Hornpipe*, Lucier's *Vespers*, and Behrman's *Runthrough*. "We were [among] the inventors," Ashley notes, "of the idea of the kind of music where you can't make a mistake. You can't play a wrong note. Everything you do is exactly what the piece calls for. No matter what you do, it's within the definition of the piece."

The earliest publicly available piece of Ashley's is a 1957 tape piece called *The Fox*, which was mixed at his home studio in Ann Arbor and is described as his first electronic piece. It is a satirical setting of a song by the 1950s folk singer Burl Ives, the lyrics altered to be a little darker. The accompaniment to the voice part is a tape of varied piano clusters, each of which has been recorded both forward and backward, with the attack cut off on both ends; the effect is a pointillist melody of pitched noises with no clear timbral identity. The poem, read in a stilted whisper, begins:

The fox went out one chilly night
He prayed to god to give him light

For he had miles and miles to go that night
Before he reached the town.

He ran till he came to the farmer's den
The ducks, the goose were kept therein
Some of you are going to grease my chin
Before I leave this town.

The Bottleman (1960), already mentioned, is a groundbreaking experimental film by Manupelli intended for two simultaneous projections, depicting in nonlinear narrative the daily journey of a poor bum who collects bottles. Ashley's forty-three-minute score mixes vocal sounds and found sounds at variously altered playback speeds into a drone created by a 60-hertz hum being picked up through contact microphones. More musically ambitious was Ashley's next tape work, *The Fourth of July* (also 1960). He had been working on a tape-loop piece using sine waves at mathematically determined frequencies but found that his scheme was beyond his technological abilities, so he improvised with the loops until he obtained a crazy mélange of rapidly swirling sine tones. About the same time, he was testing a parabolic microphone by recording the sounds of a July 4 party in his neighbor's back yard (the partiers were all friends of his). It occurred to him that the sine tones and party sounds would mix well. The piece begins with recorded boogie-woogie, chirping birds, laughing, and talking from the party, sounds that are gradually overwhelmed by the electronic sounds over the next eighteen minutes.

Soon after that came Ashley's first theater work, *Public Opinion Descends upon the Demonstrators* (1961), a prophecy of the direction his music would ultimately take. The audience is divided into sections facing different directions and is alternately bombarded with electronic sounds and left in silence. The durations of these bombardments and silences starts at thirty seconds and increases in proportions determined by the Fibonacci series (in which each pair of numbers is added to generate the next: 1, 1, 2, 3, 5, 8, and so on). During the silences, the sound controller watches the audience, and, catching any "significant" activities—these are defined in the score to include whispering, yawning, scratching, "seeking a remote visual diversion," and so on—turns on the sounds aimed toward that point in the audience. Ashley prepared six different versions of the work depending on audience size.

1. exactly 6
2. 15 to 40
3. 41 to 273

4. 274 to 12,816
5. 12,817 to 28,278,465
6. 28,278,466 or more[17]

The size of the version determines the length of the piece (the briefest performance is for the largest number of people), the types of sounds used, and the audience layout. For the smallest performance, the sound sources can be radios; for Size 2 they should be sounds of a symbolic character, like musical instruments or machines; for Size 3 they should be sounds of human activities, and so on.

The idea seems to have been to cue the audience members that during the silences they themselves were cueing the sounds and determining the shape of the piece. The musicologist H. Wiley Hitchcock, a young professor at the University of Michigan at the time, left us a wonderful picture (although Ashley finds it slightly misdescribed and insists that the piece began with sounds, not in silence) of the premiere performance in his "Current Chronicle" review for *Musical Quarterly*:

> Before it started, the audience was arranged in four blocks, each facing a different direction, so that a person in one block was necessarily looking at the group of people in another. Then Ashley seated himself at the switchboard of a series of tape-decks, snapped on a stopwatch, and began intently to scan the audience. Several minutes passed in silence. Then someone coughed nervously—whereupon Ashley pressed one of the switches in front of him, and we heard some of his electronic music (which the composer describes as striving towards "a texturally dense, restrained musical flux"). Then, silence again. Someone tittered nervously. Again, on came taped sound—different, this time, and seemingly related to the titter. More silence. Someone, angry, stood up to stomp out of the hall. A burst of angry tape music! And so on, the audience actually cuing the music by its own actions and reactions. One composer in the audience was livid with anger: "Why, he's manipulating people!" he cried. "Isn't that, in a sense, what the artist has tried to do for some time?" someone asked, but the question was swallowed up in a double salvo of taped sounds. The work ended when the stopwatch reached a certain point. By that time, some people, at least, were pleased with the peculiar effect of being able to create their own demonstration and with the interplay, not to say confusion, between "composer" and "audience."[18]

Thirteen years later Ashley would write that the piece "is about that divided consciousness I feel at concerts. I believed that the feeling could be made less ominous, that if one could accept that divided consciousness (the American Concert Consciousness), it could even be enjoyable. I think, too, we spend so much time in unreal situations (searching) that it is hard for us (Americans) to distinguish between the situation and what some other cultures might call the 'music' (what you thought you came for)."[19]

The next phase in Ashley's music would be a series of pieces in which performers would basically improvise according to strict schemata. Like much radical music from this period, the concept behind these pieces stemmed from serialism. In attempting to apply the 12-tone row concept to all aspects of music, the serialist composers had imposed independent ordering criteria on what came to be called the *parameters* of music: pitch, rhythm (or duration), timbre, and dynamics. Contrast and variety were maximized, so that, say, dynamics would range from *ppp* to *fff*, and, on balance, there would be generally the same number of notes played at each graduated dynamic level. The complexity of the systems involved resulted in music that was extremely difficult to play precisely and yet so improvisational-sounding that the precision didn't seem to matter. What was perceived was mostly the contrasting of every possible aspect of sound. Following the lead of Cage with his chance pieces, many younger composers, Ashley among them, decided that equally intriguing results could be obtained via rules that allowed for a certain amount of chance and improvisation.

The next few years, then, found Ashley writing mostly graphic scores with lengthy instructions. Instrumentalists could choose their own pitches, on the spot or by predetermination, and were to vary their *types* of sounds according to an abstract scheme. For instance, the performer might have to strive to create a pure or harmonious sonority at certain times and a noisy or dissonant one at others (as in Ashley's *in memoriam . . . CRAZY HORSE*); to contrast continuous tones with transitory ones (*in memoriam . . . JOHN SMITH*); to contrast tones in terms of pitch, intensity, timbre, and density (*in memoriam . . . ESTEBAN GOMEZ*); to choose in various sections ordinary tones versus vibrato, voice-added tones, noise, or silence (*Waiting Room*); choose at various times short, medium, and long durations (*Complete with Heat*); or make tones different in pitch when the score gives an odd number, and in timbre when an even number (*Trio* I). The concepts had resulted from serialism but were freed from serialism's exorbitant demands on the performer to execute dauntingly precise notation.

Ashley was certainly not the only composer writing scores that consisted mainly of instructions; Oliveros, Lucier, Young, Harold Budd, and many others were doing the same. Neither was he the only composer making graphic scores; Cage and Feldman had done so, and Haubenstock-Ramati made them his specialty. And the Sonic Arts Union was not the only improvisatory electronics group on the scene; AMM and Musica Elettronica Viva flourished at about the same time. But Ashley was distinctive in the extent to which his pieces were based on a social model of cooperation, with the players being required to make choices and put the piece together according to his instructions. Different as these works sound from his operas, one can draw a straight line from his graphic scores to the close collaboration with a set group of performers that his operas would require.

In 1967, in the first issue of the era's premiere avant-garde journal, *Source*, Ashley published four unconventional scores he'd made in 1961–62, his "in memoriam" pieces: *in memoriam . . . ESTEBAN GOMEZ (quartet)*, *in memoriam . . . JOHN SMITH (concerto)*, *in memoriam . . . CRAZY HORSE (symphony)*, and *in memoriam . . . KIT CARSON (opera)*. All four are named for figures who played various roles in the clash between European and Native American cultures. Esteban Gomez (c. 1483–1538) was an explorer who sought a quicker route from Spain to Asia than the journey around the Strait of Magellan and who, failing, explored the northwest coast of America in 1525 and took indigenous people back to Spain.[20] John Smith (c. 1580–1631), of course, is the English soldier who founded Jamestown, Virginia, and according to legend was saved by Pocahontas; Kit Carson (1809–68) was an American frontiersman and army scout; and Crazy Horse (d. 1877) was one of the Sioux who fought against Custer. The reason behind these choices, Ashley says, is that "it seemed from my reading of European musical history and American social history that there was a remarkably curious coincidence between the emergence of a musical form in Europe with the emergence of a very 'similar' social idea represented by the American hero. It was as if the same 'idea' happened on both continents at the same time but had to be represented differently."[21]

In the quartet, four performers decide in advance on a "reference sonority" in which the sounds of the individual instruments merge and are not distinguishable. Then, each following his or her own pulse, the performers are directed to modify their contribution to the sound by altering the pitch, loudness, tone color, and density (this last referring to the mixing of tonal ingredients, such as humming while playing, flutter-tongue, and multiphonics, or the playing of more than one pitch at a time by a solo woodwind). The concerto is for three musicians, each playing eight different instruments, with assistants who anticipate and hand them those instruments. The score is a pattern of circles aligned to an 8 × 8 grid on a piece of paper. Each performer assigns eight locations in the performance space to the vertical or horizontal lines and the eight instruments to the other. Two kinds of sounds are allowed: *continuous* ones that can be moved from location to location without interruption and *transitory* sounds, each unique to one location and instrument. The players then move around the room guided by the patterns of circles, making the required sounds.

For *in memoriam . . . CRAZY HORSE (symphony)*, the needed forces are at least five groups of wind, string, or other sustained-sound instruments, with at least four musicians per group. Each group plays from one of thirty-two pages, each containing a circle of numbered dots that refer to beats in a pulse selected by the conductor (see figure 1). Some of the radii are marked by durations; when these are reached, the group is to make a sound for the indicated duration. The group notates in advance which radii will indicate *pure* (harmonious) or *noisy* (dissonant) sonorities. Finally, the opera, for eight performers, is particularly abstract. Its score has eighty-one moments indicated by vertical lines in a grid, and instruments or performers or groups of performers indicated by the horizontal lines. Dots on the grid indicate individual events performed at the time and by the performer indicated; lines between dots represent "the direct transfer of an action or its consequences from one set of conditions (point) to another."[22] Tyranny describes the original performances as "very casual. There was a rug and a couple of couches, and people were sitting casually on the couches, or on the edge of the couch, just like something you'd encounter at someone's house. But mysterious, nevertheless."[23]

These pieces grow progressively more abstract. Reading the quartet score, one can imagine what a performance might sound like; in the concerto one imagines long and short notes contrasting; the symphony refers to pure and noisy sound complexes; and the opera refers only to events and transferred actions. In the back of the issue of *Source* in which these pieces appear is a transcript of a November 1966 conversation between Ashley, Larry Austin, and Karlheinz Stockhausen that took place in Davis, California. Ashley described the new pieces:

> I've been trying to make pieces which use the ensemble more completely, in which the ensemble determines what the person does. And the pieces I sent you were the last ones I tried to do on paper. Since then we have made pieces by working together. Just practice. You get together with an idea. You describe the idea, and everybody talks about it, and then we try to work it out. . . .
>
> By the time of a public performance all the things that have gone into it are so complex that I can't notate them any longer. I'm not very interested in other people doing these things. I don't know why.[24]

Three of these four pieces have been released on recordings. *in memoriam . . . CRAZY HORSE (symphony)* was issued on vinyl on the Advance label in 1966 with works by Mumma, Cacioppo, and Scavarda.[25] One review said, "In a manner of speaking, the music on this record is as ugly as a broiled lobster, but what a delicious taste it has for the ears!"[26]; this description could apply to much of the ONCE festivals' music. Decades later, in 1997, the New York ensemble Essential Music recorded (on the small Monroe Street label) an eight-minute excerpt of the opera *in memoriam . . . KIT CARSON*; a subdued murmur of pointillistic

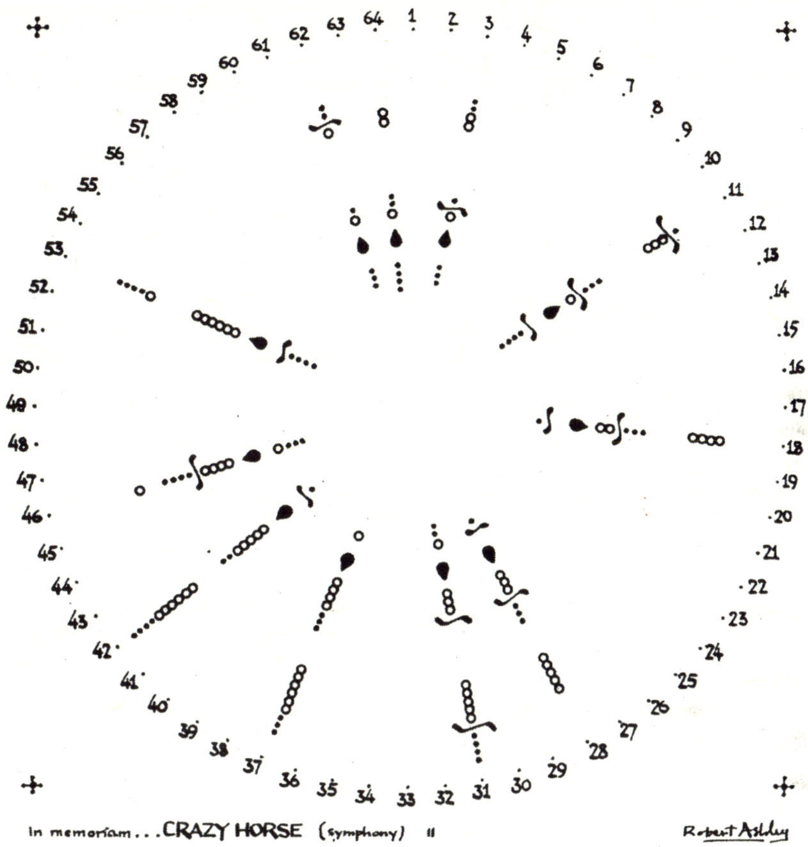

FIGURE 1. A page from *in memoriam . . . CRAZY HORSE (symphony)*

percussion crescendos into vocal yells, and it is difficult to picture what is actually happening. The quartet *in memoriam . . . ESTEBAN GOMEZ* was released on compact disc in 2007 by Ensemble MAE. They chose as their "reference sonority" a consonant drone with a prominent major third, from which subtle deviations in timbre and pitch emerge. In this reading, the piece sounds like classical minimalism.

Details (1962) is a piece for piano and two players, one on the keyboard and the other inside the piano, playing the strings. Sets of material are laid out in the score in phrases, with pitch indicated only generally as to register. Noteheads are marked as to staccato or legato; indications for the person playing the strings give ad hoc notations for strumming, plucking, thumping the string with a fingernail, and so on. The two players are supposed to respond to each other, matching each other's sounds in pitch, dynamic level, or duration, choosing freely from the materials in each phrase. *Fives*, from the same year, scored for two pianos, two percussionists, and string quintet, is based on what Ashley calls an "encyclopedia of proportions and combinations"[27] based on the numbers 1 through 5. It is a mercurial, Stockhausen-ish work that sounds like it could easily be serialized—which it is, in a sense, using only five numbers rather than twelve. Ashley would later use the same number charts to generate other pieces such as *Van Cao's Meditation* and *Outcome Inevitable*, though he has since misplaced the charts.

In 1964 Ashley produced the work with which his name would be most closely associated for decades, one of the most notorious pieces of the 1960s avant-garde. A singer in New York had asked Morton Feldman for a piece, but he didn't want to write it, so he passed on the (unpaid) commission to Ashley. Ashley didn't want to write the conventional kind of piece that would have satisfied the singer, but he agreed to write a piece anyway. He comments, "That's the way things came to pass in those grim days."[28] Ashley had been wanting to work with feedback, and this was his opportunity. He instructs that the piece be performed in an environment of loudspeakers in which the amplification is turned up to the level at which any sound entering the microphone will result in feedback.

The vocal performer is supposed to sing vocal phrases of about thirteen seconds each. The first three and last three seconds are to be held constant; during the middle seven seconds, the vocalist is to continuously alter the sound according to one, and only one, of four parameters: pitch (over one octave), loudness, vowel (moving the tongue from the back of the mouth to the front or vice versa), and closure (from lips pursed to jaw open as far as possible). Each phrase begins with the same tone with which the previous phrase ended. Ashley stresses that the tongue should be kept touching the top of the mouth, because "this particular kind of vocal cavity allows a certain amount of acoustical feedback to be present 'within' the voice," and also that the mouth should remain close to the microphone, so that the mix of vocal sounds and feedback creates an acoustical illusion of moving around the hall, depending on frequency and other factors.[29] The vocal feedback part of the piece is heard over a tape accompaniment, which can be either *The Fourth of July*, his backyard party piece from 1960, or *The Wolfman Tape*, a six-minute "blizzard of very short sounds across the whole frequency range."[30]

In addition to this rather abstract-sounding exploration of acoustics, the theatrical element of the piece, on which part of its notoriety depends, is that the vocalist is supposed to appear as a "sinister nightclub vocalist," with spotlight and in a nightclub-like space. The other source of the piece's reputation was that it was, at the time, the loudest music most of the audience had ever heard. Ashley notes that it wasn't until two years later that feedback became a common part of rock music performance and that in 1964 people weren't yet playing records and live music nearly as loudly as they would in the post-Woodstock era. So *The Wolfman* acquired a reputation as a malevolent piece that amounted to sustained torture for the audience. Twenty years later, in the symphonies for three to twelve and eventually one hundred electric guitars of Rhys Chatham and Glenn Branca and the hyperamplified sax and bass wailings of the group Borbetomagus, *The Wolfman* would be mainstreamed, if not dwarfed, in terms of its volume. But through the 1960s and 1970s, it stood out as the furthest point any musician had dared reach in the still relatively new technique of amplification.

Ashley was right that Feldman's singer friend would decline the piece. He premiered it himself on September 1, 1964, at Judson Hall as part of the First New York Festival of the Avant-Garde, organized by avant-garde cellist and performance artist Charlotte Moorman. The piece was subsequently performed in Ann Arbor and at the Walker Art Center in Minneapolis in 1965; in Los Angeles, at the University of California at Davis, in New Orleans, and at Brandeis in 1967; on tour in Oslo, Stockholm, Brussels, and London in 1969; by Ashley again at The Kitchen in New York in 1979; and in 1985 at Symphony Hall in Chicago by the Loop Group.

Ashley notes two regrets about *The Wolfman*. One is that the piece was believed to consist of someone "screaming into a microphone." In fact, he says, the vocal sounds used to induce the feedback have to be extremely soft so as not to block it, and the changes in the performer's vocal cavity are used to shape the feedback and project it to different points around the room. The other regret is that he was never able to perform the work in a room large enough to get the feedback down in the register he wanted. The smaller the room, the higher the frequency of the feedback produced, and even in a medium-sized concert hall the sound is ear-splittingly shrill. But in 1994 Ashley visited Barcelona as a tourist and happened to wander into an immense cathedral as the priest was beginning to say the Mass. The sound engineer had left the amplification on too high and had apparently gone to lunch. The priest realized the problem, but the engineer was gone, and the feedback was low enough in pitch, in about the same range as his voice, so he just went ahead. According to Ashley, "It was remarkable and beautiful, as though the priest were being accompanied by a huge, ghost choir singing Gregorian chant in exactly the key and mode that the priest was using in his singing and chanting. I realized that I was listening to a version of "The Wolfman" in a way that I would never hear again."[31]

Waiting Room (1965), originally titled *Quartet* and published as such in *Scores: An Anthology of New Music* by Roger Johnson in 1981,[32] is a characteristic graphic score for any number (its title notwithstanding) of winds and strings. The piece was commissioned by the Selmer Musical Instrument Company for their house magazine, and one wonders what they thought of the abstract-looking diagram they received. The score comprises a string of symbols of six types: filled-in circles, empty circles, circles containing three horizontal lines, circles with the latter V inside, circles with the letter N, and dots. The dot represents a silence of one breath in duration. The filled-in circle represents a short (though not staccato) sound dying away quickly. The empty circle denotes a long sound over the duration of one breath or bow. The circle with three lines calls for an exaggerated vibrato, the V for voice added to any tone, and the N for a noise. In a technique that Morton Feldman became closely associated with, the players proceed at their own pace and are not synchronized. A recording made at the March 29, 1966, ONCE concert is moody and sustained and features not only clarinet and French horns but several people reading various texts in a whisper; an extra direction allows for the presence of people reading as quietly as possible, as well as dancers who appear to be asleep among the ensemble.

The Entrance (1965) involves placing thirty-six stacks of pennies, half the stacks all heads-up and half the stacks tails-up, on the keys of a two-manual electric organ. The stacks are added to the keyboard one by one according to a simple pattern, and if any stack of pennies is spilled, it is to be reassembled before resuming. No reference is made to the sound of the organ.[33]

That Morning Thing

It is worth discussing Ashley's 1967 theater piece, or opera, if you will, *That Morning Thing*, at some length. Not only is it Ashley's most ambitious piece for the ONCE festival and the direct predecessor of *Perfect Lives*, it is the source of two of his best-known early works after *The Wolfman* and of two of his first works to be commercially recorded, *Purposeful Lady Slow Afternoon* and *She Was a Visitor*. In description, the piece sounds extremely elaborate and dependent on very specific technology. The impetus for the work was that, within a period of a few months, three of Ashley's female friends, who didn't know each other, committed suicide (one, from his own neighborhood, drove her children to school and then drove to a parking garage and jumped off the top floor). The three deaths seemed inexplicable. "*That Morning Thing*," Ashley says, "was an attempt to come to grips with that, to get rid of it, so you don't have to keep thinking about it all the time. It becomes something outside of you, a shield between you and whatever you think about it."

The title *That Morning Thing* came from Ashley's reading about suicides and learning that many take place early in the morning, around 4 or 5 A.M. "There's something about the human machine," he says, "that runs out of gas around 4 or 5 in the morning. I think the psychologists' theory was, you wake up at 4 in the morning and say, what the fuck am I doing? [Then] you really wake up a couple of hours later and reassemble yourself." The strategy was to alternate in the acts between rationality and irrationality. The opera falls into three acts and an epilogue:

1. Frogs
2. A Cool, Well-Lighted Room
3. Four Ways

Epilogue: She Was a Visitor

"Frogs" is a half-hour lecture by a man talking calmly and rationally about the possibility of nuclear holocaust. The subject matter is that nuclear waste being dumped into our rivers and streams is causing horrible mutations in the frog population, and we need to watch frogs to realize how we are potentially poisoning the human race. Behind him play four tapes of frog croaks, as though the whole thing is taking place in a swamp. Eight female dancers behind the speaker wear glasses made from automobile lights and equipped with thermal bulbs which blink. Men in the ensemble guide the women's movements (since the women can't see) by a rhythmic code, and the women hold nine-volt batteries in such a way that when they touch hands, the lights in their glasses blink.

"A Cool, Well-Lighted Room" features a woman dressed as a nightclub singer accompanied by Tyranny on the piano. She is directed to sing in an irrational (beatless) rhythm that she makes up on the spot, and Tyranny is supposed to play along until he can match her rhythm. On a screen behind them flash photos of fashionable women from magazines. The center of this act is the piece that would become *Purposeful Lady Slow Afternoon*. Ashley originally wanted four women describing in a purely factual way experiences they had gone through, but when he asked his female friends for stories, he found none of them could be sufficiently descriptive and nonpsychological. "They'd say this happened, this happened, and all of a sudden there'd be a 'because,' and you'd be out here someplace. I kept telling them, please, please. And finally, I was unsuccessful." Faced with a deadline,

Ashley wrote his own text, a kind of composite of the women's experiences, all of which turned out to be about sex.

On the 1971 Mainstream recording, ONCE member Cynthia Liddell speaks the following text in a hesitant, vulnerable voice, as other women's voices groan electronically and a glockenspiel taps out the notes of an innocent major triad:

> I remember he tried to put his gum in my mouth.
> I remember it felt afterwards like my mouth was open for the whole time.
> I remember my mouth felt stretched afterwards.
> I remember he put his tongue all along my teeth.
> He ran his tongue along my teeth on the inside and on the outside.
> When he ran his tongue along the bottom teeth it seemed natural, like a tongue.
> It felt rough.
> But when he ran it along the top teeth, he had to touch them with the bottom of his tongue and it was too smooth. . . .
> I remember one time he put his finger between my legs and got it wet and tried to put that finger in my mouth.
> I remember he put all of his fingers in my mouth and pushed down on my tongue.
> It made a lot of water come in my mouth, and he wouldn't let me swallow.
> I remember he had his tongue in my mouth and he opened his pants.
> It was awkward for him. . . .
> I remember when my face was in his pants, in the opening of his pants.
> He pushed on the back of my head.
> I remember when I had it in my mouth finally he put two fingers in the corners of my mouth with it, and stretched my mouth open.
> Then he pulled my mouth down on it.
> He pulled my mouth as if it were fitting my mouth to it.
> He pulled my head down until it touched the back of my throat.
> I choked.
> It made my throat open as if nothing were between my mouth and my stomach.
> I felt hollow.
> Then he lifted my head. Then he pushed it down again.
> I remember it was very slow.
> I remember it was like having something in my mouth that I couldn't touch.
> I got the idea.

Ashley insists that this text was tame compared to some of the stories he was actually given, but there's something about hearing it in such a simple musical context, not knowing what's going to come next, that is almost heart-stopping. In the full opera, this chilling narrative segues into another, similar improvisation with the nightclub singer and Tyranny.

In "Four Ways," the four men sit with briefcases containing microphones and loudspeakers; by opening and closing the briefcases, they modify the sounds of their voices as they describe (scripted) instances of having been too afraid of attractive women to express their attraction. Meanwhile, the solo narrator comes out, and the eight female dancers call out questions, asking directions to various locations. As the narrator answers, he points toward the locations, a kind of vernacular choreography that Ashley enjoyed.

The close of the opera consists of having the narrator repeat the words "She was a visitor" again and again. The eight dancers move out into the audience, picking up and extending the phonemes of the narrator's phrase into a sibilant continuum, sustaining each sound for one full breath. In the score for the piece, published in 1981 in Roger Johnson's *Scores: An Anthology of New Music*,[34] Ashley laid out the sounds as follows:

sh; e;	oo;	a;	z:	a;	v;	i;	z;	i;	t;	er;
She . . .	was . . .			a . . .	visitor . . .					

Ashley leaves open the possibility of having the audience participate in the sustained sounds. A recording of *She Was a Visitor* was released on a record called *Extended Voices*, produced by David Behrman and performed by Alvin Lucier conducting the Brandeis University Chamber Chorus, on the Odyssey label in 1968.[35]

For decades famous only through description, *That Morning Thing* was beautifully reconstructed at The Kitchen in New York City in November 2011. The piece originally had five performances between 1967 and 1969: two at ONCE festival concerts in Ann Arbor (February 8 and 9, 1968), one at Brandeis University in May 1968, one in Tokyo in February 1969, and one at Mills College in December 1969, where Ashley had, by then, gone to work as the director of the electronic music studio. In the Tokyo performance, Ashley finally got his four female original monologues for *Purposeful Lady*, but, since they were in Japanese, he didn't understand them; he likes to imagine that his intentions were fulfilled at last.[36]

Another of Ashley's better-known ONCE-oriented pieces is titled either *Fancy Free* or *It's There* (1969), depending on which of two texts is used. Published by Peter Garland in the first issue of *Soundings* in January 1972, the piece requires five performers: a male speaker and four cassette recorder operators. One text was written for a speaker (Alvin Lucier) who stutters, and the letter *r* in particular seemed to make Lucier stutter:

I	AM	FANCY	FREE
UNDER	A	STARRY	SKY

GREY GREYERTHAN A MOTHER'S CUNT
AND BITTERER

The other text, for *It's There*, has variants: for instance, the first line can be "Recently I've found it," "More frequently now I've found it," or "Just after waking I've found it." In either piece the speaker is supposed to read the text repeatedly, as the cassette-player operators record him. Every time he stumbles or stutters, the cassette-player operators play back the mistake, or, in the case of *It's There*, they play back any version that is not the one they expected to hear. The piece ends when an entire repetition of the text goes by without any interruption from the cassette players. The opening phoneme of each word is built up gradually, the word drawn out slowly, and words are to be separated by four to eight seconds. In the case of imperfections, cassette operator 1 is supposed to play back only the offending syllable, operator 2 the word, operator 3 the line, and operator 4 the entire text, so that a counterpoint of time scales overlaps beneath the speaking voice.[37]

ONCE Group Compositions

The eventual demise of the ONCE festivals was rooted in resistance to the increasing theatricality and provocativeness of the ONCE Group's larger projects. At the September 1965 festival, called ONCE AGAIN, the group took over the roof of the Maynard Street Parking Garage for a collaborative work titled *Unmarked Interchange*. The 1935 Fred Astaire film *Top Hat* was projected on a film screen made up of independently movable panels. Vertical louvers in the screen opened and closed, revealing a couple eating watermelon and drinking champagne, people in a large drawer reading a play, or Gordon Mumma reading the famous erotic novel *The Story of O*. A weather balloon emerged from the screen and floated away. Carolyn Cohen walked across the screen and threw a pie into Mumma's face. A pianist played Grieg on an upright piano. Meanwhile Ashley controlled the audio from a console behind the audience, emphasizing now one event and now another.[38]

As already clear from *That Morning Thing*, some of the more provocative ONCE Group pieces explored uncomfortable areas of male-female relationships. One of these was Ashley's *Kittyhawk* (1964, premiered in 1965 in St. Louis). In it the men maneuvered the women into positions of danger, such as walking across a high plank blindfolded or being tied to a suspended board. The climax took place in a blackout in which the audience was directed to throw paper airplanes at the stage, which, once the light returned, was revealed to contain only a woman taped to a wall. Ashley's title alludes to the beginnings of aviation as well as to the dichotomy between kitties (women) and hawks (men). His subtitle, "An Anti-Gravity Piece," as well as the description he published in the 1965 *Tulane Drama Review*, makes the piece seem like an abstract exercise, with no allusion to the rather unmistakable, explosive political subtext.[39]

Such pieces made the Dramatic Arts Committee wonder whether their money was being spent on worthwhile projects. One group composition called *Night Train*, performed at Brandeis in 1967, so disoriented the audience with collage elements and sexually suggestive language that they threw food at the performers. Richard S. James has argued that *Nighttrain* merely made visible the internal pressures that were already beginning to rip the ONCE Group apart.[40] However that may be, at some point Wilfrid Kaplan called Ashley to a meeting and told him that he was pulling his support; he had close friends in the university's music department, and they were skeptical about what was going on. Relations with the music department had started out well but had cooled after some percussion instruments borrowed by ONCE musicians had been ill-treated. Ashley recalls that at one concert at which David Tudor played underneath the piano and John Cage played turntables, the entire university music faculty stood up en masse and walked out. Ultimately, the music department killed the ONCE festivals, though perhaps at a point at which their joyous creativity was beginning to take a darker turn.

Nevertheless, there was enough benign energy left for one last ambitious extravaganza: Ashley's theater piece *The Trial of Anne Opie Wehrer and Unknown Accomplices for Crimes Against Humanity* (1968). In this work, Wehrer sat with her back to the audience and answered one hundred questions portentously taped in advance and coming from loudspeakers. Two additional inquisitors (Joseph Wehrer and George Manupelli) cross-examined her answers, and they in turn were answered by two surrogates (Mary Ashley and Cynthia Liddell). Some of the questions seemed invasively personal; others were meant to draw out Wehrer's connections with famous people she had known:

22. What diseases have you had?
23. Do you smoke, drink, or habitually use any narcotic?
33. Your name is listed on the program of the 1948 Bachelors Cotillion in Baltimore, Maryland. Please describe this event and your participation in it, using as many names of persons involved, as you are able to remember.
35. Please characterize, briefly, but as frankly as you can, the following persons, regardless of whether you know them personally.

Frank Sinatra
Stokely Carmichael
Mrs. Robert Kennedy

38. Please describe the most distasteful thing you have ever done for money.
42. Have you ever kissed a woman for sexual reasons?

Wehrer was apparently a magnificent conversationalist (Ashley says he once listened to her talk for fourteen hours nonstop), and the results were allegedly riveting. The piece seems like a trial run for the interrogations Ashley would work into his later operas, particularly *Improvement* and *eL/Aficionado*. In addition to the ONCE festival performances, the ONCE Group gave other variously staged performances of *The Trial* in Sheboygan, Wisconsin; La Jolla, California; Colorado Springs; and New York, one of them with just Ashley and Wehrer as a duo.[41] The questions played too slowly to get through all of them in one performance, and each new performance would just pick up wherever the last had left off.

During the heady ONCE festival years Ashley worked at first in the reference department of the University of Michigan library, a job he enjoyed and was good at; he remembers impressing his boss by finding out for a customer the gross national product of Indonesia between 1952 and 1954 in two minutes. Because he couldn't get anyone to cover his absence when he went to Venice with the Space Theater, he had to quit the job. Upon his return, Anne Wehrer introduced him to someone who was producing industrial films for the Detroit auto industry. In 1964 he formed a little company called Robert Ashley Sound, and for six years he made soundtracks for what he calls propaganda films. As he recalled in an interview, "There'd be a movie about shock absorbers. . . . These movies were all designed to go to the guys who owned the sales lots. Chevrolet made tons of 16mm movies and sent them to everyone who sold Chevrolets. So the guys could have a staff meeting, and it would clear up their ideas about whether the Pinto would actually explode and burst into flames if you ran into it from behind. . . . We'd make movies that said that didn't really happen." While he would occasionally write original music for these, he hated doing so, and preferred matching up films with pre-existing music or sounds. Around 1969, however, Detroit started losing business to Japanese and European automakers, and demand for Ashley's business went into decline. Luckily, it was in that same year that he got a call from Mills College in Oakland, California, asking him to set up an electronic music studio for it.

One final post-ONCE project is yet to be mentioned, one that gives some hint of the style of ONCE Group activities: the *Dr. Chicago* films. Between 1968 and 1971 George Manupelli made three films (actually four, but one was destroyed in a fit of resentment) based on the character Dr. Chicago, an outrageously self-regarding sex-change quack, the name an obvious take-off on Boris Pasternak's *Dr. Zhivago* and the epic 1965 film that had recently been based on it. Alvin Lucier, and his famous stutter, starred as Alvin Chicago, and the plots revolved around his adventures on the lam for medical malpractice as he heads for Sweden to open the Dr. Chicago Medical Center. Lucier clearly improvises his monologue throughout the films, often with hilarious results, listened to by a quiet and strangely passive Sheila Marie (played by Mary Ashley). Dancer Steve Paxton co-stars as a mute sacrificial-saint character who gets killed in every film. The second film, *Ride, Dr. Chicago, Ride*, features the composer Pauline Oliveros as a laconic old West–style accordion player in the desert. Ashley made the rather minimal soundtracks and is credited as one of the writers, but as he would later write, "There were many occasions when people working on the films sat around the night before, without Manupelli present, and made up scenes and jokes which would turn up in the performance the next day."[42] Absurdist and variably brilliant, the *Dr. Chicago* films give us little specific insight into Ashley, but they are an invaluable late window on the ONCE Group personnel, their collaborative methods, and their existential humor.

4 Incredibly Slowly Our View Begins to Slide

The Mills College Years

IN THE 1960S MILLS COLLEGE WAS a women's college, and on the undergraduate level it remains so today. The head of the composition program was the distinguished French composer Darius Milhaud (1892–1974), best known for having made some of the first use of jazz style in European music in his *La creation du monde* (1923). In 1940 Milhaud, a Jew, was hastily exiting France prior to the arrival of the Nazis when he received a telegram offering him a teaching job,[1] at the insistence of Mills alumna and wealthy new-music patron Elizabeth Sprague Coolidge. He accepted. Though confined to a wheelchair by rheumatoid arthritis, Milhaud divided his post-war time between Mills and Paris. His idea at Mills was to have a concert each semester, with new European music (including his own), plus that of an American composer, in each.

In the mid-1960s, partly in response to Milhaud's presence, Mills received a Rockefeller Grant to start a contemporary music program. Part of this program would be a Tape Music Center to make Mills competitive in the new electronic arena. In 1966 Pauline Oliveros was hired to direct it, but she received a better job offer the next year at the University of California at San Diego. Local composers Lowell Cross and Tony Gnazzo replaced her but soon left. Roger Reynolds was asked, but he had also already taken a job at UCSD. He recommended

Ashley. So, in the fall of 1969, Ashley moved to Oakland, California, with Mary and Sam. He also insisted on bringing with him both "Blue" Gene Tyranny and Ann Arbor electronics expert Nick Bertoni, and Mills acquiesced. This odyssey would become the opening setup for the opera *Foreign Experiences*.

Ashley and Bertoni built a five-section studio with a recording studio, a tape library, a tape-editing studio, an instrument-building workroom, and a Moog synthesizer studio and were allowed by Margaret Lyon, chair of the music department, to knock down walls and reconfigure the space as they wanted. Since there was not yet a teaching program to encourage Mills's undergraduates to use the studio, Ashley had the idea of making it a public-access facility that local musicians could use. Ashley called his program officer friend Howard Klein at the Rockefeller Foundation and successfully asked for funding for the project. For ten dollars an hour, local bands and artists could use the studios and have either Ashley's student Maggi Payne or Tyranny as a studio technician. (Born in Texas and educated at Northwestern University, Payne arrived at Mills in 1970 as Ashley's first student; she remains there on the faculty to this day.) The program was a tremendous success. Partly because of his fundraising skills, Ashley was invited, after two years of building the studio, to stay on as a professor. He accepted, on condition that he be given tenure. "I never thought of myself as a teacher," Ashley writes today. "Teachers had mostly been the bane of my musical existence."[2] (Milhaud retired the year Ashley joined the faculty, 1971.)

Ashley started Mills's coeducational master's degree program in electronic music, still a prestigious program today, and changed the departmental emphasis from concerts of famous composers to having each student give a concert every year. He taught courses titled Introduction to Electronic Music Performance, Selected Problems in Composition, and Seminar in Electronic Music, all of them two-semester courses.[3] As best he could in new circumstances, he continued the kind of activities he had directed in Ann Arbor. His last unfulfilled plan for ONCE had been a seventy-two-hour festival. He and Bertoni finally succeeded in doing this at Mills, bringing in musicians from all over the country. The climax of it, as he recalls, was a performance by Maggi Payne, who played the flute with a plane circling overhead. She stood on a mound of earth; as the plane broadcast a recording of Nelson Eddy and Jeanette MacDonald singing "Indian Love Song," Payne answered each phrase of the recording with her flute. Ashley would frequently bring composers in to speak to his class. (Incidentally, Ashley never met Harry Partch, who performed in the Bay Area occasionally, but he did meet Lou Harrison a few times.) In addition to Payne, many of Ashley's students from Mills went on to musical careers, including Paul DeMarinis, Laetitia Sonami, John Bischoff, and the composer known as Fast Forward.

Despite this new and promising life on the West Coast, it was a depressing period for Ashley. His composing had slowed to a standstill, and he had no plans to continue. With the demise of ONCE, nobody, he felt, was interested in his kind of music, and he didn't want to just write music that would sit in a file cabinet. One reason for his discouragement was reading in 1968 about the Shiraz Arts Festival, lavishly funded from 1967 to 1977 by the Shah of Iran at the insistence or his worldly wife Farah Diba; the festival poured millions of dollars into productions of works by Stockhausen, Iannis Xenakis, Cage, and Merce Cunningham, and Ashley couldn't imagine his music ever being supported at that level. (Artists who participated, however, risked being heavily criticized for collaborating with a repressive regime.)[4] In addition, Ashley's marriage, as marriages sometimes will, had gone on the rocks; Ashley and Mary separated in 1972. (Mary would develop early-onset Alzheimer's disease and die in 1996.) For six years he lived alone in what he invariably refers to, even in his operas, as a "shitty apartment" a block from the Mills College studio.

The fallow period in Ashley's work list lasts from 1968 to 1972. During that time, according to his records, he completed only a few film music assignments, *Fancy Free* (described in chapter 3) and an odd but compelling theater piece titled *Morton Feldman Says* (1970), which consists of a dialogue between Ashley and Feldman with Feldman speaking in his inimitable style. The dialogue was taken from a series of interviews Ashley did with Feldman in 1965. (Ashley was considering writing a book about Feldman, which never materialized.)

In 1972, however, Ashley's muse caught a second breath. He started with a kind of audio-opera whose origins sound like a story in one of his operas. In 1957 a poet friend of his named Keith Waldrop (b. 1932), while getting a Ph.D. in comparative literature at the University of Michigan, came across an odd little volume titled *In Sara, Mencken, Christ and Beethoven There Were Men and Women* by John Barton Wolgamot. It was a collection of 128 versions of the same sentence, varying primarily in what proper names and adverbs appeared. For instance, the book begins:

> In its very truly great manners of Ludwig van Beethoven very heroically the very cruelly ancestral death of Sara Powell Haardt had very ironically come amongst his very really grand men and women to Rafael Sabatini, George Ade, Margaret Storm Jameson, Ford Madox Hueffer, Jean-Jacques Bernard, Louis Bromfield, Friedrich Wilhelm Nietzsche and Helen Brown Norden very titanically.

The eighth sentence reads:

> In their very truly great manners of Teodor Jozef Konrad Korzeniowski very heroically Gertrude Allain Mary McBrady and John Barton Wolgamot had very sardonically come amongst his very really grand men and women to Gamaliel Bradford, Anne Green, William Hervey Allen, Jr., Washington Irving, Pierre Corneille, Arthur Schnitzler, Mari Sandoz, St. John Greer Ervine and Herman Melville very titanically.

And so on and so on. A kind of cult following for this odd little book grew among the ONCE members until finally, in 1972, Ashley decided he had to use it as a basis for a piece of music. (As Waldrop recounts in an essay for the liner notes of the recording, Ashley wrote him and said that he had written no music for a few years because he had been "purifying himself." "'Now,' he said, 'I am pure.'")[5]

Ashley found that he could read through an entire sentence of Wolgamot's book in a single breath, but, of course, would then have to pause for a deep breath for the next sentence. To create a continuous vocal texture, he simply recorded every sentence and ran them together on tape. He had one of his students at the time, Paul DeMarinis, design a series of synthesizer configurations that could be correlated to the appearances of the special names that occurred most often in the text: Henry Louis Mencken, Jesus Christ, William Shakespeare, Sara Powell Haardt (Mencken's bride late in life), and so on. The piece *In Sara, Mencken, Christ and Beethoven There Were Men and Women* was released on vinyl on the Italian CRAMPS label in 1974 and re-released on Lovely Music in 2002. Though not high-energy, it is nevertheless a forty-minute relentless onslaught of words, names, and popping synthesized burbles.

Meanwhile, through a series of chance encounters and variously successful queries, Waldrop and Ashley actually met the reclusive Wolgamot in 1973. Ashley learned that Wolgamot had conceived the piece when he heard an outdoor performance of Beethoven's *Eroica* Symphony in New York and started hearing people's names in the work's rhythms—names he eventually confirmed to his own satisfaction by reading a biography of the composer. To make a long and curious story short (the reader is referred to the extensive liner notes of the Lovely Music disc), Ashley got to know Wolgamot in the late 1970s and learned how deliberate and detailed his methods were, how each page was painstakingly crafted to paint a particular picture. For instance, as Ashley explains, on a page that contains the names Paul Gauguin, Oland Russell, Harley Granville-Barker, Somerset Maugham, and others, "Somerset has both summer and set as in sunset, and Maugham sounds like the name of a South Pacific island, and Maugham wrote a biography of Gauguin, which name has both 'go' and 'again' in it, and

Oland could be 'Oh, land,' a sailor's cry, and Granville sounds French for a big city, which Gauguin left to go to the South Pacific."[6] Suffice it to say that Wolgamot's long proper-name prose poem fit hand in glove with Ashley's view of language as music and that Ashley found something kindred in Wolgamot's obsessive devotion to a highly disciplined and enigmatic task.

A spin-off from this piece was Ashley's only string quartet, titled *String Quartet Describing the Motion of Large Real Bodies* (1972). The piece was conceived as accompaniment for a possible opera based on Wolgamot's book, but as with some of Ashley's other works from this period, the plan was impractical, involving as it did as many as forty-two electronic musicians altering the sound made by the four string players. The amplified string players were to make "a stream of intentional but unpremeditated (that is, random) very short sounds" by pulling a heavily rosined bow very slowly across a single string. These signals were electronically delayed en route to the loudspeakers and triggered by coincidences between the original and delayed sounds. This prickly, reverberant, and rather minimalist piece was released on the Italian record label Alma Marghen in 1999 (in a rough draft version with a single violin), along with a piece called *How Can I Tell the Difference?*, which used as a sound source a motorcycle traveling through a concrete tunnel near San Francisco.

During this period Ashley met Mimi Johnson (b. 1946), director of an organization called Performing Artservices. A native of Galesburg, Illinois, Mimi had gone, after college graduation, to live with an aunt and uncle in Paris—the painter and novelist Dorothea Tanning (b. 1910) and her husband, the famous surrealist painter Max Ernst (1891–1976)—and, through their connections, work as an intern in an art gallery. There Johnson's mentor was the formidable Bénédicte Pesle, who managed a wide range of artists and who directed the European careers of John Cage and Merce Cunningham, as well as many other famous figures. In the summer of 1970 Pesle placed Mimi in a go-fer job on a Merce Cunningham Dance tour, where she met Cunningham's troupe composer, Gordon Mumma, and, at a 1971 tour date in Brussels, also met his friend Robert Ashley. That year Johnson returned to the United States, where avant-garde arts activity was noticeably on the rise, and formed Performing Artservices as a branch of Pesle's international work; John Cage had already offered to be a client, and Johnson became his manager for the rest of his life. Mumma and Johnson were in a loose relationship, but by the spring of 1973 Ashley had succeeded in spiriting her away and was totally in love. She lived in New York, so Ashley would regularly take the red-eye flight ($199 round trip) from San Francisco. In 1979 Mimi pried him out of the "shitty apartment" and into the Lake Merritt hotel, a beautiful Art Noveau building from the 1920s next to Lake Merritt in Oakland, designed for rich people from San Francisco to stay on their summer vacations. The hotel was empty much of the time, and Ashley was, as he puts it, "their star customer."

Now Ashley's muse returned with a vengeance. Having been so successful at organizing huge events in Ann Arbor and at Mills, he thought of staging a two-month residency in which various composers would come through. Each would stay a few days, talk to Ashley about various things, and stop to perform their own music from time to time. Eventually the idea arose to videotape the whole thing. As Ashley went on sabbatical in 1975, this videotape idea grew into the status of an opera, with the composers as characters, playing themselves and providing different musics through their different speaking styles. On a trip to New York, Ashley consulted his friend at the Rockefeller Foundation, Howard Klein, and told him he was looking for funding to do a major opera—"opera" in the totally unconventional ONCE festival sense. At this time, 1975, opera was considered a stodgy, moribund classical music genre; the next year, Glass's *Einstein on the Beach* would begin to change all that by offering a paradigm for a new, hipper definition. But in 1975, Ashley recalls, Klein told him, "If I said the word 'opera' to my board of directors, I'd be fired."

Ashley returned to California discouraged. However, once there he told his friend Bill Farley about his ideas. Farley suggested, "What's hot right now is video documentaries. Don't tell the Rockefeller Foundation it's an opera. Tell them it's a video documentary." Ashley wrote to Klein to ask about funding for a series of video documentaries, and Klein wrote back, "Send me a budget"—meaning, in Ashley's experience, that the idea was accepted. The Rockefeller Foundation offered $25,000, and Klein suggested that Ashley also appeal to the Ford Foundation; soon Ashley had a large budget to work with.

Music with Roots in the Aether is a series of seven video interviews, each an hour long, and each followed by a one-hour performance of the composer's music. The composers are David Behrman, Philip Glass, Alvin Lucier, Gordon Mumma, Pauline Oliveros, Terry Riley, and Ashley himself. What makes it an artistic video work is in part the amazing creativity of Philip Makanna's camera work and visual scenography, which embed the interviews in overarching theatrical processes. (Ashley had already made two soundtracks for Makanna: *Battery Davis*, 1970, and *Shoot the Whale*, 1971.) As Ashley wrote in the foreword to the book accompanying the video:

> The interviews themselves are casual and desultory. They had to be, because of the manner in which they were made. They were made in front of a video camera, with the rule that there would be no video editing. So, the composers are just talking. . . . Such a plan

> carries no argument with it. It makes, at best, a kind of splintered portrait of a few people whose lives and whose work I admire. It is almost coincidental to this intent that these same people have contributed individually and collectively to so much of what is the shape of serious music in 1999, not just in America now, but wherever American music is heard.[7]

The interviews themselves are "shattered," as Ashley describes them, but, almost casually, the presentation is shaped into a wonderfully artistic whole. For Ashley, language is music, and the interviews, spotty, rambling, and dotted with thoughtful silences as they are, form one line through the counterpoint of ambient sounds, wistful images, and ongoing visual and audio transformations.

For instance, the Philip Glass segment takes place in a pure white space with no apparent boundaries. Ashley starts talking about his fear of children; Glass says he's comfortable with children. After several minutes of conversation, children start marching by in the background, back and forth, as Glass and Ashley talk on unconcerned, and finally the children are playing in the background, the camera sometimes panning to focus on them as the conversation continues. Eventually the background fills with children, the susurrus of their play becoming the video's ambient soundtrack. The background changes gradually from pure white to the mottled colors of the children's clothing. The interview takes place within a gradual, disarmingly natural visual and audio process. The interview was filmed at a small Manhattan television studio, and Ashley had asked a friend to lead her daughter's second-grade class over during the interview—without warning Glass, who looks a trifle surprised, but who plays along.

Some of the oddest pleasures here stem from the effect of the separation of sound and image. The Behrman video begins with the camera moving rapidly over San Francisco Bay and Behrman saying, "We certainly have a bird's-eye view of our surroundings now, Bob. . . . Imagine, this is where we live. It's hard to believe." The mind assumes that the voices come from people on the boat, but then the "boat" rises and soars over the city of San Francisco—it is actually a helicopter, though we can hear no propeller noise. Eventually it flies until we see in the distance two men sitting at a picnic table; it zooms toward them, landing with a slight jostling of the camera. The two men, of course, are Behrman and Ashley, whose unflappable conversation we've been hearing all along, and it continues with no notice of the arriving helicopter. The Mumma interview takes place in two chairs in the middle of an empty football stadium; he rides in on a bicycle, and he and Ashley discuss electronic instruments as folk instruments.

The Ashley contribution contains two theatrical pieces, *What She Thinks* and *Title Withdrawn*, and no interview. *What She Thinks* is a fascinating midpoint between the ONCE festival aesthetic and the upcoming *Perfect Lives*, containing hints of both. On a stage festooned with red, white, and blue ribbon, Mimi Johnson is dressed up like Whistler's mother and holding a microphone. Ashley is wearing an unlifelike white wig and is identified by a caption as George Washington ("the father of his country"). "Blue" Gene Tyranny is made up as a moody Beethoven ("the father of modern music") and sits at a piano rather manically trying out variations on the theme of the *Eroica* Symphony. DeMarinis, in a spotless white suit, is Guglielmo Marconi ("the father of mass communications"), working away at a synthesizer. Captions scroll by giving information about the historical figures portrayed, not all of it correct (for instance, it is said that Marconi would be 198 years old by that time, when actually he would have been 102).

Title Withdrawn requires a little more explanation. Ashley is convinced that he has a mild form of Tourette's Syndrome. In his younger years, this took the form of his sometimes having to leave a gathering to find privacy and repeat words over and over, profanities or phrases like "you guys are all." He connected this to making music both in the sense of needing to make sound and also "trying to get something right." He tried for years to use his involuntary speech creatively but could never (by definition) produce it at will, as a performance. As he puts it, "I spent years tinkering with my consciousness trying to reconcile the performer—legal and highly paid—with the person you cross the street to avoid."[8] Finally he rigged up a recording setup in the Mills electronic studio during a long period in which he wouldn't be disturbed and succeeded in making a forty-five-minute tape of intermittent but compulsive and repetitive speech whose content, when he played it back, surprised him as much as it would have anyone else. For years he didn't know what to do with the tape, but, analyzing it, he found a quality of "fourness" to the voice—words in groups of four or four repetitions—and eventually decided it needed to be combined with three other characters. In the end he added Mimi's voice, whispering a French translation of his own words, some burbling electronics from a Moog synthesizer, and a gentle, even nostalgic improvisation on an electric organ. This work, in its audio format, was titled *Automatic Writing*.

Title Withdrawn, the video piece included in *Music with Roots in the Aether*, uses *Automatic Writing* as its soundtrack. The video image seems unconnected with the music, unless one knows sign language. It is actually two signers from the California School for the Deaf signing the words from *Automatic Writing* as displayed (off-camera) on cue cards. The pair's almost-but-not-exactly parallel motions, sometimes only partly within the camera frame, make a curious microtheater.

Following the sabbatical, Ashley realized that he didn't want to go back to Mills, especially because he wanted to be in New York with Mimi. He arranged to teach only one semester a year from that point and asked David Behrman if he wanted to take the alternate semesters. In 1978 Ashley and Mimi got a tip from Kurt Munkasci, Philip Glass's sound engineer (who still lives in the building), about a large loft space in an old building in Tribeca, on Manhattan's Lower West Side, that had started as a meat-packing plant and that was being sold for an attractive price; *Tribeca* is a local term taken from the phrase "the triangle below Canal Street." Ashley and Mimi borrowed money from Mimi's mother and bought the sixth-floor loft to live in; today Ashley uses it as a studio. In 1986 they also bought the fourth floor and moved into it as their living space. In 1981 Ashley would finally quit Mills College, whose electronic studio was taken over by his friend David Rosenboom.

Meanwhile, in 1977, the amazing cameraman of the *Aether* videos, Philip Makanna, stepped forward with a new suggestion. His favorite movie was *The Wizard of Oz*, and he conceived the idea of filming a contemporary remake of it. He suggested that Ashley write the story. (Thus the lines in *Foreign Experiences* and *Celestial Excursions* about Ashley's becoming a screenplay writer at this point in his life.) This attempt to do so made Ashley begin taking seriously the idea of writing his own narratives; until this point, he had written the occasional text for a ONCE piece, but then it would be worked on collaboratively. Now he was coming up for the first time with his own characters and plots. "I discovered," he says, "that I couldn't think of an idea unless it came out of my mouth. I can't sit down at a typewriter and write a story, I had to *tell* the story, talking to myself."[9]

The working title for the film was *Famous in a Certain Sense*. At some point, however, it dawned on Ashley that Makanna was never going to produce the movie and that he had to transform it into something he could perform himself. Meanwhile, Mimi was starting a record company that would become the Lovely Music label, and she pressed Ashley for a recording she could produce. At this point he had only two characters defined, an older man at the beginning and a young woman at the end: these would eventually become Raoul de Noget at the beginning of *Perfect Lives* and Isolde at the end. (How this evolved from an updating of *The Wizard of Oz* I leave to the reader's imagination.) He had one scene, "The Park," for the older man, and one called "The Backyard" for the woman. He auditioned Mimi to read one of them; she tried and said, "Absolutely not." He auditioned others but couldn't get anyone to capture the sense of subtly metered rhythm that he had in mind. Finally, in some impatience, he set up a microphone in the Mills studio and read the text straight through himself. He discovered that he liked the effect. Another character he had had in mind was called The World's Greatest Piano Player, so he asked Tyranny to come in and try playing along with the recording of his voice. Tyranny came up with several different piano characterizations in the style of Liberace and other well-known pianists. They settled on one style that would give Tyranny the most freedom to improvise.

Next Ashley added a drone line to the recording of his voice. He knew of a local sitar player, Krishna Bhatt (b. 1949), who later recorded with Terry Riley. Bhatt also played tabla, and Ashley hired him to provide a tabla accompaniment. Bhatt didn't want to be known for playing the tabla, a lower-caste instrument in Indian music, so he forbade his name to be used; he is credited on the recording only as Kris. (At this point, Ashley hadn't yet worked out the ideas for having each scene in a different meter; this would come later.) Ashley instructed Bhatt to listen to the recordings and play something that would match his voice. Bhatt did so, and then they recorded; Ashley astounded Bhatt by being so delighted with the results that they quit after one take. Afterward, Tyranny went into the studio and, listening through headphones to the tape of the tabla, Ashley's voice, and the drone, added a piano track. And thus was produced, in 1977, the soon-to-be-famous vinyl recording of the first and last scenes of *Perfect Lives*, which, in its first incarnation, was titled *Private Parts* (affectionately referred to by fans, following the advent of the more elaborate version of *Perfect Lives*, as "the yellow record").

Although he had performed excerpts earlier, the premiere performance of this early Ashley-Tyranny version of *Perfect Lives* in its entirety took place October 24, 1979, at Northwestern University, where Ashley had been invited by faculty composer Peter Gena. Back in those early days Ashley would read the text—he has never required his opera performers to memorize—from a video screen, as a backstage assistant flipped index cards inscribed with the text in front of a video camera. At that first complete performance, I was the assistant flipping the text cards. I was a graduate composition student of Gena's at Northwestern, already a longtime Ashley fan, and eager to help. (That I would someday analyze the piece in a book seems almost fated.) Those spare, spellbinding first performances consisted simply of Ashley reading, Tyranny playing the piano, and a background tape of drones and drumbeats to keep time.

Lovely Music's second Ashley release, *Automatic Writing*, came out on vinyl in 1979. As abstractly as Ashley now thinks of the piece in terms of "fourness" and the unnotatable rhythm of involuntary speech, the listener to the pure audio version receives a much more cinematic impression. For decades the Moog sounds have always sounded to me exactly like rusty bedsprings creaking gently, and Ashley's occasionally intelligible murmuring, Mimi's sultry whispering (echoing Ashley's words in French), and the soft organ add up to a luxuriantly erotic sound picture, the audio track to a happy postcoital scene in an invisible movie. (The album cover, a picture of palm trees silhouetted against a night sky as through a window—an image from the video—hardly contradicts the impression.) At the end, the other "characters" even die away to let the organ finish with a withheld cadence, a suspension that perversely refuses to resolve. Alfred Hitchcock's train going into a tunnel could hardly be more explicit. Ashley and Mimi were married, by the way, on August 24, 1979.

Ted Hariton (*left*) and Robert Ashley (*right*), ca. 1938.

Ashley family photograph. Used by permission.

Anne Ward, Diane, and Robert Ashley, ca. 1948.

Ashley family photograph. Used by permission.

Diane, Anne Ward, and Nancy Ashley, ca. 1948.

Ashley family photograph. Used by permission.

ONCE Group and Judson Dance Theater members, ca. 1965.
(*left to right, front*: Yvonne Rainer, Joseph Wehrer, Robert Ashley, unknown man, George Manupelli; *middle*: George Kleis, David Bates, Gordon Mumma, Meredith Monk, Cindy Liddell; *top*: unknown man (standing), unknown woman (standing), Jackie Leuzinger, Annina Nosei, Phoebe Neville (?); *background*: unknown man, Caroline Blunt, unknown man.)

Photograph by Makepeace Tsao. Used by permission of Performing Artservices, Inc.

Alvin Lucier, Robert Ashley, and Anne Koren during the performance and video recording of "Outlines of Persons and Things" for *Music with Roots in the Aether.* 1975.

Photograph by Philip Makanna. Used by permission of Performing Artservices, Inc.

Robert Ashley, New York. 1980.

Photograph by Michael O'Brien. Used by permission of Performing Artservices, Inc.

Robert Ashley in *Atalanta (Acts of God)*. 1985.

Photograph by Bruno Bruni. Used by permission of Performing Artservices, Inc.

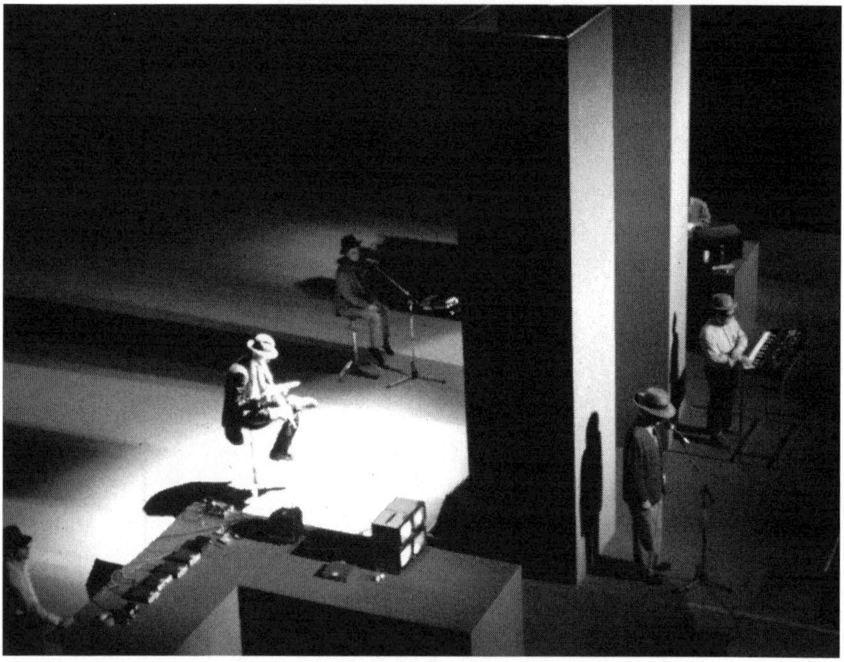

Atalanta (Acts of God) at the Centre Georges Pompidou, Paris. 1982.

Photograph by Lawrence Brickman. Used by permission of Performing Artservices, Inc.

Robert Ashley in *Concrete*. 2009.

Photograph by Hiroyuki Ito. Used by permission of Performing Artservices, Inc.

Robert Ashley in *Dust*. 2008.

Photograph by Marco Caselli Nirmal. Used by permission of Performing Artservices, Inc.

Robert Ashley in *Celestial Excursions*. 2003.

Photograph by Mimi Johnson. Used by permission of Performing Artservices, Inc.

Robert Ashley at the Coconino County Fairgrounds, Flagstaff, Arizona. 2009.

Photograph by Mimi Johnson. Used by permission of Performing Artservices, Inc.

5

I'm Not the Same Person That I Used to Be

Perfect Lives

AT THIS PIVOTAL POINT WE WILL DO WELL to generalize about Ashley's mature conception of opera from *Perfect Lives* on. It is a completely individual conception: no other composer has ever shared it, though some younger ones (including "Blue" Gene Tyranny and Mikel Rouse) have been influenced by it. Ashley himself has been extremely articulate in describing it. Starting with *Perfect Lives* he began to conceive a great trilogy of operas—*Atalanta*, *Perfect Lives*, *Now Eleanor's Idea*—that would form a kind of history of American consciousness. In time, *Now Eleanor's Idea* would break up into four different operas. The total of six operas were conceived, he says,

> as a television series, with each episode having some meaning and humor in itself, but ultimately part of a larger something that only makes sense when you come to know it. Television devotees who have watched *The Honeymooners* [a classic television show from 1955–56, starring Jackie Gleason, aired in reruns for decades] for most of their lives finally come to know something that they wouldn't know if they had only seen one episode. Same for *Star Trek* [a popular science fiction show, 1966–69].These were my models. I have had to compromise the form of the presentation of my operas, because I was not able to get into television. But they are pure television. They are meant to be heard and seen by two people sitting on a couch, having a drink, occasionally a snack, occasionally going to the toilet, finally giving up and going to bed because of a hard day of work. They are meant to

be seen many times. The details pile up, and finally there is a glimmer of the larger idea. This is my idea of opera.[1]

Ashley's operas have plots, and (as, frankly, with any conventional European opera) it is helpful to know the plot in advance, as it is not necessarily decipherable from the text alone. Each opera is based on a plot, but Ashley freely admits that probably no listener would be able to recount the plot from having listened to the opera. Plot, he writes, "requires a lot of 'exposition.' We have to keep being reminded of what is happening. I don't have time to do that, and it's not interesting to work on." What the listener will take away afterward, he believes, is a vivid memory of the central character and some dialogue.[2] (The author can attest that entire paragraphs of Ashley's dialogue often stick in the mind with no effort required on the listener's part. The turns of phrase are just that vividly surprising.) Much of the plot remains in the background.

Elsewhere, Ashley makes a distinction between plot and storytelling:

> At the opera I am transported to a place and time where there is no disorder. There is disorder on stage, and it is called melodrama. We don't believe it. This is important: that we don't believe it. We do believe . . . what happens in the movies. . . . Therefore, opera can have no plot. It is foolish to argue that opera—any opera—can have a plot; that is, that the "characters" and their apparent "actions" and the apparent "consequences" are related in any way. Opera can be story-telling only. That the story-telling happens on stage and that musicians are making music in the pit (to reinforce the story told) is entirely coincidental. The story might as well be told at the kitchen table with a crazy aunt and uncle as the soprano and tenor.[3]

Because Ashley's texts are not immediately understandable in a linear way, they have been called stream-of-consciousness, but as he has also written, "I have taken a lot of heat about 'stream-of-consciousness' writing from critics who apparently have read a book about modern literature and who can't hear or don't have time to listen. There is no 'stream of consciousness' writing in my librettos. The texts are all purposeful, rhetorical 'structures' based on the musical templates. That they are not as easy to understand and put together in a 'plot' as something from *Reader's Digest* doesn't surprise me at all."[4] Let the listener take this to heart. In the context of his stories, Ashley's librettos make sense, but the complete sense may hinge on taking in considerable background extrinsic to the work itself.

Likewise, Ashley's operas do not have a conventionally musical score. The basis of an Ashley opera score is the text written out, line by line, with the lines numbered. Each line might represent (usually, from *Atalanta* on) a three-beat measure or a four-beat measure. Generally, the accented syllables are underlined so the performer can quickly grasp how the phrase fits into the measure, though this is somewhat loosely applied. Harmonic changes and changes of reciting tones for the various voices are often noted on the appropriate line. Sometimes, especially for the self-contained "pop songs" found in each opera, a specific melodic tune might be notated in the margin. Improvisation rules or a chord progression that moves too fast to fit within the line sequence might be noted at the bottom of the page.

There is no such thing as a "typical" Ashley score, because (1) different operas specify different information, and (2) within one production, different scores are used for different purposes—the singers, for example, don't need to see the same information as the sound engineer. But the page from *Foreign Experiences* given in figure 2 can be taken as emblematic of the kind of information the scores contain. On the left are listed the singers for each line (with corrections made in rehearsal). The next column is the line count, which in some cases the singers are hearing through headphones to keep on track. Next is the line itself; this act uses a four-beat line, and the accented syllables are underlined. An underlined slash (or in

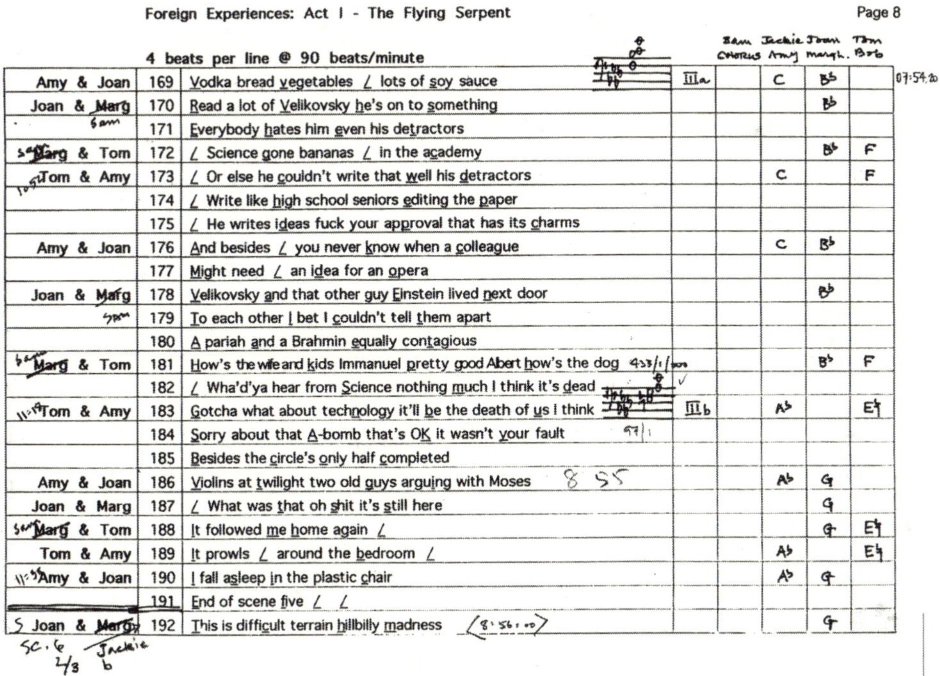

Foreign Experiences: Act I - The Flying Serpent — Page 8

4 beats per line @ 90 beats/minute

Amy & Joan	169	Vodka bread vegetables ∠ lots of soy sauce	IIIa		C	B♭	
Joan & Marg	170	Read a lot of Velikovsky he's on to something				B♭	
	171	Everybody hates him even his detractors					
Marg & Tom	172	∠ Science gone bananas ∠ in the academy				B♭	F
Tom & Amy	173	∠ Or else he couldn't write that well his detractors			C		F
	174	∠ Write like high school seniors editing the paper					
	175	∠ He writes ideas fuck your approval that has its charms					
Amy & Joan	176	And besides ∠ you never know when a colleague			C	B♭	
	177	Might need ∠ an idea for an opera					
Joan & Marg	178	Velikovsky and that other guy Einstein lived next door				B♭	
	179	To each other I bet I couldn't tell them apart					
	180	A pariah and a Brahmin equally contagious					
Marg & Tom	181	How's the wife and kids Immanuel pretty good Albert how's the dog				B♭	F
	182	∠ Wha'd'ya hear from Science nothing much I think it's dead					
Tom & Amy	183	Gotcha what about technology it'll be the death of us I think	IIIb		A♭		E♮
	184	Sorry about that A-bomb that's OK it wasn't your fault					
	185	Besides the circle's only half completed					
Amy & Joan	186	Violins at twilight two old guys arguing with Moses			A♭	G	
Joan & Marg	187	∠ What was that oh shit it's still here				G	
Marg & Tom	188	It followed me home again ∠				G	E♮
Tom & Amy	189	It prowls ∠ around the bedroom ∠			A♭		E♮
Amy & Joan	190	I fall asleep in the plastic chair			A♭	G	
	191	End of scene five ∠ ∠					
Joan & Marg	192	This is difficult terrain hillbilly madness				G	

FIGURE 2. A page from *Foreign Experiences*

other scores an asterisk) indicates a rest or silence on the accent or downbeat, perhaps creating a syncopation. To the right of this column are shown the chords used in the music; the first one is carried over from the previous page, and then there is a chord change at line 183. The chords are labeled according to Ashley's harmonic scheme as shown in the next column, and the last four columns indicate the changing reciting tones sung by the four performers (although they do not limit themselves to these pitches).

The score represents all the information the performers need. It does not represent the entire piece. What Ashley calls "the orchestra"—the instrumental music that is played digitally behind the speaking characters—is built up layer by layer, and in some cases never notated at all. Some of the instrumental parts—for instance, the keyboard parts from *Improvement*—can be retrieved from the MIDI files and reconstructed in notation. Other elements, like the Piano Sonata recording in *Foreign Experiences* and the interview with the lowrider in *Now Eleanor's Idea*, are just audio artifacts. Creating a new performance of one of these operas would involve singers' performing from the score over the recorded backgrounds. In some cases, the "orchestra" could be replicated using newer technology, and much of the information necessary for this would have to be obtained by ear. Ashley is open to the idea. In fact, the Lovely Music recording of *Foreign Experiences* was produced by Sam Ashley with newer technology and using only two voices (his own and Jacqueline Humbert's) instead of the original seven.

The singing technique used in these works is not what people expect from opera, and it constitutes a large part of the resistance to considering them opera. In general, the lines are sung on and around a kind of reciting pitch, what Ashley calls a "'character-defining' pitch (that is, a pitch somewhere in the singer's range that, understandably, forces a certain 'character' to emerge)."[5] The singers inflect the text around this pitch, guided by the harmonies notated in the score, and frequently break into a freer speech pattern. Occasionally adjunct pitches are notated; in some cases (notably *eL/Aficionado* and act 4 of *Now Eleanor's Idea*) scales are given to improvise on. Some of the text is spoken with a conversational flow, while some words are accentuated in notatable rhythms.

What qualities from Ashley's music for the ONCE group are found in the operas, and what devices enabled him to pivot into a style and genre so discontinuous? Ashley's mature operas fit a layer of narrative into a kind of conceptual framework not too different from his music for the ONCE festivals. Often an empty time structure based on an unvarying pulse is involved. For instance, *in memoriam . . . CRAZY HORSE (symphony)* is based on a variable pulse determined by the conductor, in which sounds happen at predetermined moments. Likewise, in *Perfect Lives*, *Atalanta*, and the *Now Eleanor's Idea* operas (except for *Foreign Experiences*), the pulse is ♩ = 72 beats per minute (bpm) throughout, and all the musical and textual events are keyed to various points in this pulsed continuum. The idea of time as a preset empty space to be filled was an idea developed by John Cage in his music of the 1940s and 1950s, and Ashley accepts it as almost self-evident. As *Public Opinion Descends upon the Demonstrators* is structured in advance according to time lengths based on the Fibonacci series (regardless of what happens in performance), the operas *Improvement*, *Foreign Experiences*, and *Now Eleanor's Idea* are all based on symmetrical divisions of a 6,336-beat template.

Ashley's first six operas to follow *Music with Roots in the Aether* all involve the same characters. For Ashley, *Atalanta*, *Perfect Lives*, and the four separate operas of *Now Eleanor's Idea* form a vast trilogy more than ten hours in duration. Respectively, they represent the past, present, and future, and, therefore, three phases in human history: architecture, agriculture, and genealogy. They also represent a geographical America divided by two mountain ranges: the past east of the Appalachians, the present between the Appalachians and the Rocky Mountains, and the future west of the Rockies. As Ashley stated when he was still conceiving the overall structure:

> [T]he plot I have in my mind is that the three operas, *Atalanta*, *Perfect Lives*, *Now Eleanor's Idea*, would represent the history of our consciousness as Americans. The first of the operas, *Atalanta*, is obviously derived from the oldest of the European myths; it's the earliest form of the American consciousness, with its *European* roots—excluding the Black American consciousness, or Indian American consciousness—I'm just talking about white American Judeo-Christian consciousness. The first one is our European roots; it's the earliest in chronology, and it's also fundamental in the structure, it's what we started from. The second of the operas, *Perfect Lives*[,] is placed in a later historical time when for everybody in the United States, their sense of roots is being eroded. A time when people are not so much thinking about their European roots, they are thinking about their relationship to their environment, to other Americans, to their contemporaries. *Now Eleanor's Idea*, the last of those, is predictive. I'm actually trying to go as far as I can into the future, with what the American consciousness might evolve to, as one might go to the past to see where it came from.[6]

Perfect Lives

For many listeners, *Perfect Lives* remains Ashley's best-known and most emblematic work. The characters in *Perfect Lives* include Raoul de Noget, a singer who's seen better days, and his pal Buddy, "the world's greatest piano player"; Isolde, an unmarried woman nearing thirty and her brother D (for Donny), the captain of the football team and also assistant to the bank manager; six tellers at the local bank, named Gwyn, Jennifer, Kate, Eleanor, Linda, and Susie; old-timers Helen and John, who live in "The Home"; Rodney, the bartender, and his wife Baby; the bank manager; Ed and Dwayne, friends of D's; Isolde's father Will, the sheriff, and his wife Ida; and a justice of the peace. Isolde and D involve Raoul and Buddy in their scheme to commit the perfect crime: to steal all the money from the bank for one day and let the "whole world know that it was missing." Meanwhile, Ed and Gwyn are going to Indiana to elope, so D plans to put the money in Ed's car.

The plan is for Raoul, Buddy, and Isolde to go into the bank, Buddy with his dogs, which create a ruckus. Isolde will take a bucket of water from next door to throw at the dogs but will miss and throw it on the bank manager, who will go into the vault to change his clothes and discover that "the bank has no money in the bank." Isolde has also called her father Will, disguising her voice, to draw him to a decoy, a nonexistent accident out on the highway. The dogfight takes place at 12:45 P.M., and each of the tellers has a different experience of it; in a kind of *Rashomon* effect, these different points of view will be expanded into other entire operas. Raoul and Buddy retire to the bar afterward and meet Rodney, who eyes them with suspicion. Will and Ida figure out the plot, too late, and Ed and Gwyn, unaware of the bank money in their car, find a justice of the peace to marry them.

There are seven episodes in *Perfect Lives*: "The Park (Privacy Rules)," "The Supermarket (Famous People)," "The Bank (Victimless Crime)," "The Bar (Differences)," "The Living Room (The Solutions)," "The Church (After the Fact)," and "The Backyard (T' Be Continued)." Since this is an opera for television, each episode is intended to be 24 minutes and 40 seconds in length, which in 1979 was the legal minimum length of a television half-hour, allowing for commercials. (Actually, during the corporate-friendly Reagan administration that length was further reduced to 22 minutes, making *Perfect Lives* impossible for American television in its intended format. However, Ashley received an offer to produce the opera for Channel 4 in Great Britain, where the commercial half-hour was 25:50. It was for this purpose that, in the video version but not the Lovely Music recording, he added on the title sequences with stories that open each episode.)[7] The tempo in every act (and in some of Ashley's subsequent operas as well) is always 72 bpm. Each act has its own rhythmic and visual template to distinguish it from the others. The seven metrical templates are as follows:

Scene:	*Beats per line:*
Park	13 (8+5)
Supermarket	5

Bank	9 (5+4, 4+5, alternating when the narrative jumps to the future)
Bar	7 (4+3, 3+4, depending on whether Buddy or Raoul is speaking)
Living Room	4 (in triplets)
Church	4
Backyard	triplet in 5- and 4-beat lines

As Ashley writes, explaining the effect of his time signatures,

> We were in asymmetrical times—13, 5, 9, 7—for the first four pieces. Obviously, then, we had run out of asymmetrical times, there just weren't any more [though one wonders why 11 was excluded]. For the next three pieces we either had to go backwards and repeat those times, or go in some other direction. . . . The thing about symmetrical times for long songs—that is, songs that last about a half-hour—is that asymmetrical time is very very beautiful. The coincidences are so weak, the actual structural cadences are so ephemeral, that you can just go on forever. I mean, if you get things going in say, thirteen, there is no time . . . whereas if you do things in 4s, or 2s, or 6s, it becomes very heavy. . . . You can't stay out there on the stage for two and half hours if everything is going 4/4, it makes you crazy. You have to think of a way that it's interesting for you spiritually. Otherwise you might as well be driving a car.[8]

As the listener quickly realizes, these rhythmic patterns are not articulated with slavish obviousness. Some of them are subtle, like the 13-beat pattern Tyranny marks in the bass at the beginning of "The Park" with his oom-pah pattern (oom-pah, oom-pah, oom-pah, oom-pah, oom-pah, oom-pah, oom / oom-pah, oom-pah, and so on). There are several more or less obvious 7-beat ostinatos (repeating melodies or chord sequences) in "The Bar," including the one that runs from 22:25 to 24:06 on the CD recording—lightly disguised because its ambiguous first beat sounds interpretable as an upbeat. Elsewhere, however, the line length is often creatively obscured by cross-rhythms or static textural patterns. It is an underlying structural principle not allowed to become monotonous.

The visual templates, by which images are arranged on the video screen for each act, are as follows:

Park	low horizontal line
Supermarket	a pyramid of lines converging at the top
Bank	a grid, with the view tilted upward
Bar	vertical lines
Living Room	screen divided in half vertically or obliquely, not horizontally
Church	a circle in the center of the screen
Backyard	a doorway splitting the screen into thirds and leading upward

Much of the harmonic shaping of the work was done by "Blue" Gene Tyranny, who played the organ and piano parts. According to Kevin Holm-Hudson, who interviewed Tyranny in 1992, when his memory of the production was fresher, each scene has a central reference pitch around which its harmonies revolve:

Park	D
Supermarket	F
Bank	A♭
Bar	D for Rodney, G for Buddy
Living Room	E♭
Church	A
Backyard	G

This doesn't mean that the scene will necessarily sound like that pitch is the tonic in the usual musical sense, for Tyranny works modally, rotating different modes around the pitch given. For instance, in "The Park," the mode is D Ionian (major) from 0:00 to 3:18 on the 1983 CD recording (1:13 to 4:33 on the video), and then switches to D Dorian—the F♯ and C♯ are lowered to F and C. From 9:23 to 13:28 (or 10:36 to 14:41 on the video), Tyranny emphasizes the ii chord in D, so that a repeated E seems to displace D as the "tonic" or at least the pedal point; that E continues as a pivot note through the next three-minute section, which uses a split mode between D minor and A minor. But at almost any point one will find that the reference pitches given appear in the harmony or at least the scale used in that scene.[9]

Like all great poetry, *Perfect Lives* is resistant to paraphrase. Ideas from books Ashley has read ripple through it and are alluded to without explanation, let alone proof. In the bibliography accompanying the libretto, Ashley lists three books as relevant to his story. Two of them are about Giordano Bruno and written by Frances Yates: *The Art of Memory* and *Giordano Bruno and the Hermetic Tradition*. The other is W. Y. Evans-Wentz's translation of *The Tibetan Book of the Dead*. The latter—more correctly called the *Bardo Thödol* in Tibetan, *Bardo* referring to the liminal passage between this life and the afterlife, *Thödol* referring to liberation through hearing—is a set of scriptures attributed to the eighth-century guru Padma Sambhava and long kept secret. Among other things, the scriptures are meant to be read into the ear of a dying person to help liberate him from the cycle of birth, death, and reincarnation.[10] According to Lama Govinda, in words Ashley echoes in the opera, the "illusoriness of death comes from the identification of the individual with his temporal, transitory form, whether physical, emotional, or mental, whence arise the mistaken notion that there exists a personal, separate egohood of one's own, and the fear of losing it."[11] The Tibetan scriptures describe various deities and colored lights that the dying person will encounter, warning him which ones to follow and which ones to shun to achieve liberation. On one level Ashley identifies the characters in *Perfect Lives* with these deities. As he once told me, "If I'm shouting into someone's ear over the microphone—that's sort of what I'm doing—I'm warning them about these characters."[12]

The one who listens to Ashley's operas needs to have the story in his mind, a story not always clearly outlined in the text itself. It also helps, in taking in his multiple levels of meaning, to know the books that form his intellectual background, whose phrases sometimes spill into the dialogue. Ultimately, however, while Ashley's words embody, and have their origin in, meaning, in the end, for us—as the libretto tells us—they are arrangements of sound. There is often little one can do to explain them besides quoting them.

A note on different recorded versions: as mentioned, the original 1977 vinyl recording of the first and last scenes (still bearing the earlier risqué title *Private Parts*) has only Ashley's voice over a background of organ chords, tabla, and Tyranny's piano. By the time of the fuller 1983 version, released on CD and video, Ashley had added many more layers to the piece, including percussionist-composer David Van Tieghem (b. 1955) and rock singer (and former Ashley student at Mills) Jill Kroesen (b. 1949) as chorus and occasional characters, to a point that sometimes verges on "information overload," a popular term in 1960s psychology that had worked its way into avant-garde music and theater. Pop aspects of the musical background are provided by Peter Gordon (b. 1951), a rock musician best known as leader of the Love of Life Orchestra. Ashley further teamed up with video artist John Sanborn (b. 1954), at the time an artist in residence at WNET in New York (he would go on to work in commercial video, including work with the rock group The Residents), to achieve his dream of a full video production of the opera. The team traveled to Mimi Johnson's family home in Galesburg, Illinois, to shoot video on and around the farm of a friend of her father's, a cattle dealer. (Mimi's father is also the George Johnson described in one of the video-version introductions, who says, "If that's the way it's gotta be, that's the way it's gotta be.") *Perfect Lives* remains, to this day, Ashey's only opera to reach the video form for which he intends all of them. The costs are too prohibitive, the society we live in too apathetic.

"THE PARK (PRIVACY RULES)"

The words of *Perfect Lives* are highly visual, often drawing pictures, which we may or may not see on the screen. The video opens with the horizon of a cornfield providing the low horizontal line; it will return as the bed of Raoul's motel room and the lower edge of Tyranny's piano. Raoul is sitting in his motel room, "unhappy with the world," introspective and unconfident:[13]

He takes himself seriously.
Motel rooms have lost their punch for him.
The feeling is expressed in bags.
There are two, and inside those two there are two more. . . .
One of the bags contains
a bottle of liquor.
A sure sign of thoughtfulness
about who one might have been.
He pours himself a small drink in a fluted
plastic glass sans ice.
He thinks to himself, if I were from the bigtown
I would be calm and debonair.
The bigtown
doesn't send its riffraff out. (6)

As noted, Tyranny's oom-pah piano beat marks off the music in leisurely 13-beat phrases; each spoken double line occupies one of those phrases. We see Buddy/Tyranny's fingers making slow glissandi up the keyboard, we see Ashley talking, and occasionally we see Ashley, as Raoul, sitting on the bed and filling the fluted plastic glass.

A description of Raoul includes what may be the first meditation on masturbation in the history of opera:

He handles himself in the morning.
It's just like for every other man.
The fantasy is the distance,
the reluctance, the reticence, the otherness.
The fantasy is the uncleanness.
So, getting up gets to be a problem for
a sensitive person like him. (9)

Raoul thinks about the contradiction between his inward rebelliousness and outward solicitousness as he tries to be helpful in filling out his request for the following day's breakfast ("Room service, courtesy of the company"). He is apparently looking at a photograph, which the text describes in detail, of two men sitting on a bench in the park of a small Midwestern town. The men philosophically divide existence into the permanent and the impermanent, assigning to the transitory category all things physical and mental:

Among those particulars which were neither physical nor mental they listed
attainment, aging, and coincidence.
On the permanent side of this great division of reality was a notion

they referred to as space.
And by that term they meant neither conceptual space
nor space
as given by our senses.
They meant connections. (14–15)

Raoul's idea is that "the transition always takes one by surprise"; he "imagines absolute awareness on the other side." Poetically, Ashley has merged the transition of change as the camera moves across the image with Raoul's imagining what death is like. The original *Private Parts* recording says that Raoul "wonders, as we all do / how it comes to you that you are dead"; the *Perfect Lives* revision changes this to "how it comes to you that the light has changed," closer in spirit to the *Tibetan Book of the Dead* and the opera's underlying theme of reincarnation.

"THE SUPERMARKET (FAMOUS PEOPLE)"

"The Supermarket" is about Helen and John, an elderly couple who live in the local old-folks' home, and who will be innocent bystanders to the bank ruckus. The text is somewhat less straightforward, and we gather information about them little by little. Toward the end of the act, the scene we find them in is described: far away in the aisle of a grocery store, the shelves converge in the perspective to form the virtual pyramid that is the visual leitmotif for this section (also given by the piano keyboard seen in extreme close-up from one end and a road whose parallels converge at the horizon). Also explained at the end is that Helen and John are in love and want to marry, but one of the rules of the home is that residents can have no immediate family by marriage, so they can't marry or they will "lose the privileges." Instead, once a week they take adjoining rooms at a nearby motel to be together.

Chord changes in the perky keyboard accompaniment subtly outline the five-beat meter. In much of the second half (13:25 to 20:15 on the CD recording) the meter goes unmarked as Tyranny indulges in a more dissonant and free-form improvisation, kept very soft. At six points (0:59, 3:45, 6:31, 10:22, 19:42, and 23:01) Kroesen echoes three-syllable phrases from Ashley's text in groups of six, in recurring refrains on the pitches F, A♭, and C, the last repetition always merging into a dying-away glissando:

welcome home
dressed in red
told and told (23)

Finally the scene concludes with a long series of these echoes.

"THE BANK (VICTIMLESS CRIME)"

After these two poem-like musings, "The Bank" comes as a relative burst of action. The speed of the text increases considerably. The nine-beat pattern is not very apparent, but over a high-energy pop drum beat Tyranny alternates between a five-beat ostinato in some passages and four-beat boogie-woogie passages in others. We hear about Gwyn, one of the bank tellers, who has told her boss that she's sick, or rather, "feels a sickness coming on. Even the Bank Manager gets it then." She's playing sick, and she gets in "the car that's full of holes" to run off to Indiana with D (Donnie), Ed, and Dwayne. At five points (on the CD, at 2:51, 4:36, 8:51, 18:18, and 22:52) she clicks on the radio and a pop song comes on, the first of many self-contained songs that will dot Ashley's operas:

> *I love-d you like an old time melody*
> *I love-d you like a dot dot dot symphony*
> *Music bringing back a memory becomes the time*
> *stops another treasury I say*
> *Oh my I say what a shame I say what did I do*
> *I say who's to blame I say I love-*
> *d you an-d an' then I call-d your name an'*
> *I say I would do it again* (58–59)

The action surrounding the bank robbery is not exactly described but alluded to:

> Where the eddies of our demodulation fill The Bank *(around 12:45, remember that!)* And in The Bank at that time,
> there is a commotion, as they say, the Manager is soaking wet. The
> older sister of his assistant *(there by chance?)*
> missed the dogfight with the bucket from next door, and soaked him.
> Everybody's laughing. *That's a relief.*
> And it has been discovered that
> the money is not there. (41)

Ed is eloping with Gwyn, and D indulges an admiring reverie about how changed Gwen will seem for him:

> Gwyn is so beautiful wrapped in danger.
> She is wrapped in scarves against the wind and noise, and wrapped in the
> danger of her under-
> taking. . . .
> We go out together, the four of us, the four of us
> planning to change things, to rearrange things among us so that for ever after,
> when I talk to Gwyn, or when Dwayne talks to Gwyn,

there will always be the scarves hiding the smiles, and no longer ever or
ever, for me or Dwayne, will Gwyn be naked in the
Summer dress. When we get back from this one, those days are gone forever,
the days of Gwyn naked in the Summer dress are gone for me and Dwayne. (42)

There are echoes in all this of Ashley's high-school exploits with the tough guy who wanted to marry his sister; Ed brings D along because he likes talking to him about theosophy and vegetarianism, and just as Ashley's theosophist vegetarian friend married his sister, Ed marries Gwyn, to whom the narrator is attracted.

The act's second half returns to the bank and introduces the five tellers who are still there, Jennifer (introduced at 13:28), Kate (14:22), Eleanor (15:21), Linda (16:09), and Susie (17:12). This part is less crucial to the rest of *Perfect Lives* than to the operas that come afterward, because the *Now Eleanor's Idea* tetralogy is linked to their experiences. Jennifer dreams while she's at the bank window. Kate is the girlfriend of the man who installed the bank's security cameras and who reads palms. Eleanor has been at the bank longer than the other girls, and one night last year lost presumably her virginity ("or, maybe, exchanged one thing that has no currency / for another that has no currency") to D. Linda is told by Kate's palm-reading boyfriend that she'll have one child, named Junior Jr., with her husband Junior. Susie's an opera fan. Three of the girls saw different aspects of the post-robbery action: Susie noticed the behavior of the dogs; Linda was intrigued by Buddy, the Mexican, if indeed he is Mexican; Kate noticed another suspicious man, presumably Raoul. Of course, the action was caught on Kate's boyfriend's cameras, but somehow "the closer you watch, the less you see." The act closes with a two-minute return of the pop song.

"THE BAR (DIFFERENCES)"

The commotion over, Raoul and Buddy retire to the local bar "after a successful day at work / Not exactly *at* the office, but at work." The text, but not the video, starts with a visual:

This is a close up.
An arm.
Big muscles
Gone to seed.
It moves.
But first,
We read,
Rodney.

The design
Looks Chinese.
Flashpowder
Tattoo. (63)

Rodney is the bartender, worn down with care over his wife Baby, who paid good money for boogie-woogie lessons at the music store with little result. "Around us in the bar," the narrator intones, "we hear the sounds of life," and Ashley's appreciation of vernacular speech as music becomes palpable:

I say,
Don't you read the Bible, man?
And: *Place like that'll make your*
Skin loose.
And: *You never know where they are*
On this portable equipment.
And: *Just one more time, then*
Put it in the joke museum.
And: *She wanted her savings and*
Whatever she could get on credit. I said,
Ma'm, it's not my neck, but what can an old fart like you
Do with all this money on a Friday morning? (65–66)

Buddy, sensing Rodney's badly veiled distrust, tries to ingratiate himself with a wonderful lecture on Buddhist understanding of the Self, which would be utterly out of place in an average bar but somehow (and underlined with a syncopated, seven-beat ostinato) makes sense in Ashley's world of creatures from the *Tibetan Book of the Dead*:

There is only one Self. That Self is
Light. The Self is ageless.
The body has four forms, times,
Eras, four ages.
But the Self the one and only Self is ageless,
Without age and without aging.
The Self is without coincidence, being
The only thing the self.
The Self is without attainment,
Being perfect. . . .
The word eternal is a mystery to me.
I don't understand that word.
I can't say the Self is ageless
Being eternal,

So, I have to find another way of seeing, another way of
    Understanding that the Self is ageless,
'N the way I've found that works for me is,
    I say: Im-
agine the Self shaving for the first time:
    No. Im-
agine the Self learning to walk.
    No.
So, the Self must be as ageless
    As it feels. (69, 72)

Rodney's dismissive remark "We don't serve fine wine in half pints, Buddy" is, to Buddy's cosmic awareness, the sound of God, but Rodney is not impressed.

This is the scene of *Perfect Lives* in which the sense of rhythmic structure is most palpable. For about fourteen minutes (of twenty-five, particularly the long section following 5:48 on the CD recording, which contains the lecture on the Self) Tyranny plays melodic or harmonic ostinatos that emphasize the seven-beat meter. Often the ingenuity with which he quietly subverts boogie-woogie patterns into this odd meter is especially delightful. The second half of the act continues and generalizes Buddy's paean to the Self, commends the alcohol that enables his eloquence on the subject, and ends with a meditation on television as industry, quoting again the act's opening words as though (as in *Finnegans Wake*) the text were circular.

"THE LIVING ROOM (THE SOLUTIONS)"

The next scene is almost entirely a dialogue between the sheriff, Will, and his wife Ida. Much of the background music is quiet, even absent in certain passages; the harmonies are relatively static, and the conversation is dotted with spoken stage directions of "(long pause)." The rhythmic scheme here is four beats in triplets, which effectively means that Tyranny's occasional ostinatos spell out a tempo of ♩♩ = 48 (since the eighth note at 144 remains the same as in ♩ = 72).

Ida asks questions relating to the temporary bank robbery, and while some of Will's answers are germane, others are non sequiturs leading to a wide range of topics. The question "Why do people swear?" starts an explanation of Tourette's Syndrome—the condition Ashley believed he had, which started his work on *Perfect Lives*. Sometimes Ashley's own persona breaks into the narrative, as in the subsequent composerly complaint about someone who called to commission him to write some incidental music, eliciting an obscene response. Will speaks from a cosmic viewpoint:

> *she says:* ' s it possible there was no money to begin with?
> *he says:* anything is possible . . . but the fact is:
> for one whole day it was gone. it was there. 'n then it was gone. 'n
> then it was back. unchanged. *she says:*
> are you investigating the chances of an inside job? *he says:*
> if we're all in this together, all jobs're inside jobs. (98–99)

Will figures out the four people behind the robbery: the seedy-looking older guy (Raoul) must be the mastermind, the "mexican" Buddy ("there's no doubt the mexican is in it. the doubt is if he's mexican"), and two locals, one of whom knows that the bank has a secret sound code that opens the safe and that is transmitted to the bank manager by a phone call from the diner. The recording of this scene ends in an unusual manner with a rather repetitive four-minute instrumental interlude.

"THE CHURCH (AFTER THE FACT)"

Ed, Gwyn, Dwayne, and D have arrived in Indiana to find Noel Givens, the justice of the peace. Teenage jokes fly around, such as the one about Gwyn's friend Snowdrift, so nicknamed because "in winter in your car at night it was easy / To get in her." (The character is based on the high school friend of Ashley's who was left abandoned at the church altar.) But this is serious business, and this scene is a sermon that takes on the whole history of humankind. The density of words has reached its climax in this passage, and Gwyn is in a suitably spiritual mood:

> Those jokes don't bother me, Your Honor. I am
> Transparent to the wishes of my Lord. I am put here and it
> Pleases me to serve Him. My soul feasts upon the rising
> Of the sun. It is His presence. The great arc of the day is
> The truth of my life. I learn from it, and am humble in
> That knowledge. And in the evening my body sleeps. (111)

A new character, Lucille, whose hair is the color of the sunset and falls in splendor, approaches the congregation (at which point we suddenly realize we are no longer in the justice of the peace's office next to his bedroom) and has the cake attached to her. (Lucille, who will reappear in *Dust*, is based on a homeless person who lived in Tribeca Park and whom Ashley came to think of as *Perfect Lives*'s guardian angel.[14] The scene with Lucille approaching the congregation and being attached to the cake is copied from a 1965 piece written for the ONCE Group, *Combination Wedding and Funeral*.) The marriage sermon is composed of rules:

1. Don't talk to yourself
2. Speak only when you're spoken to
3. Make sense

"Don't talk to yourself" is a reminder that talk isn't a part of understanding but, rather, a habit, an arrangement of sounds. The arrangement requires a partner, and thus, historically, marriage followed conversation as, in Ashley's cosmology, religion followed agriculture. "Don't talk to yourself" means stop arranging things when you're alone, and do not use for yourself what belongs to all of us: sounds. "Speak only when you're spoken to" represents the dilemma of the second historical eon, in which humankind struggled to reconcile its arrangements of marriage and religion, leading to the third eon, in which we make sense: "we have accomplished ourselves, / (*Or invented man*, as The Philosopher says)." Though the theory of history is here assumed rather than spelled out, we get some of Ashley's clearest statements of the epistemology behind his operatic use of language:

Language	has sense built in. It's easy to
Make sense.	To make no sense is possible,
But hard.	Language does not have truth built in.
It's hard	to make truth, which is to stop the search. (121)

And there is an inferred eon prior to "Don't talk to yourself," in which the arrangement of sound "may have been prior to the arrangement of sounds as / *An experience* external to ourselves, or as an experience / *Of something external* to ourselves."[15] Here Ashley refers to ideas from Julian Jaynes's 1976 book *The Origin of Consciousness in the Breakdown of the Bicameral Mind*, in which Jaynes argues that ancient man believed in the gods because his left and right brain hemispheres had not yet been integrated, and he was interpreting verbal messages from the right hemisphere as voices outside himself. Thus marriage and religion form part of the attempt to control the arrangement of sounds in the transition from the voices of gods to Tourette's Syndrome, and Ed and Gwyn, by getting married, are doing their part in this evolutionary ritual whose meaning is still unfolding.

"The Church" ends with a meditation on Lucille, embodiment of famous marriages, the passer-on of ritual whose eye the narrator catches as she brushes off the cake crumbs and leaves the church. Ashley himself breaks into the fictional narrative with a real-life event:

(This is an interruption. Now listen carefully.
What I'm telling you is true. While I am typing this, whatever it is,
The phone rings. Iris, from downstairs, wants to use the

> Typewriter. This is the first I have worked on this account in almost
> Six months. It was hard to start. . . .
> . . . So what is the meaning of Iris? She's not
> Too far from Lucille. . . .
> Maybe I'm not supposed to be telling this. I mean
> The part about passing it on.) Where were we? (129–30)

Lucille is wearing a parka whose hood, in Ashley's eye, is a halo. Lucille, for Ashley, has to do with the passing down of culture; Iris, calling from downstairs, symbolically tries to prevent the revelation of secrets. Perhaps complementing the density and complexity of the text, the musical structure is the simplest in the opera, a series of harmonies in 4/4 meter over which Tyranny improvises lyrically.

"THE BACKYARD (T' BE CONTINUED)"

The marriage of Ed and Gwyn, and Will's halting realizations about the conspirators, are the only resolutions of the action that *Perfect Lives* gives us. Now we are in the backyard of Isolde's mother's house, where friends have gathered for an evening picnic, and from whose doorway (her appearance framed by the doorway connecting her to Lucille and Iris) the unmarried Isolde counts the days. A return is made to the slower word pacing of "The Park"—a nice symmetry exhibited in their pairing on the first Lovely Music vinyl recording. The instrumental background alternates between five- and four-beat phrases in triplets at 48 dotted-quarter notes to the minute.[16] The accompaniment is rather dry and lightly drum-studded in the five-beat sections, and Tyranny limns the four-beat passages with languidly nostalgic arpeggios.

Isolde's musings are a Buddhist meditation:

> My mind turns to my breath, one.
> My mind watches my breath, two.
> My mind turns and watches my breath, three.
> My mind turns and faces my breath, four. (136)

Isolde contemplates the world from the standpoint of eternity. Boogie-woogie remains: "For her piano playing is the only mystery. / It's so beautiful, and how they do it no one knows."[17] She muses on numbers, which stretch as if made of rubber. Forty-two plus twenty can be sixty as well as sixty-two. "Giordano Bruno comes to mind, whoever he is." She focuses on the everyday phrases spoken by her friends at the picnic. For her, "Carl's still president over at the bank, ain't he?" is the sound of God, just as "We don't serve fine wine in half-pints, Buddy" was in "The Bar." As the barn swallows gather, the sun goes down, and the close of consciousness represented in the *Tibetan Book of the Dead* is symbolized by a series of the official definitions of different stages of twilight:

> Sundown, one, the time it disappears.
> Gloaming, two, the twilight, dusk.
> Crepuscle, the twilight, three, dusk.
> Twilight, four, pale purplish blue to pale violet, lighter than dusk blue.
> Civil twilight, until the sun is up to six degrees
> below horizon, enough light on clear days for ordinary occupations.
> Nautical twilight, until the sun is up to twelve degrees below horizon.
> Astronomical twilight, until the sun is eighteen degrees down,
> more or less.
> Clair de lune, five, greener and paler than dusk.
> Dusk, six, redder and darker than clair de lune. (145–46)

And finally, Isolde asks, "Dear George, what's going on? / I'm not the same person that I used to be." The dissolution of personality, death, reincarnation, the sunset, the end of the picnic, the end of the story, the letting go of worldly things, the ceasing to care about the bank robbery, the passing on of marriage to Ed and Gwyn, the end of Gwyn naked in the summer dress—all these merge into one of the most beautiful and profound passages that opera has ever offered. Yet the scene's subtitle is "T' Be Continued," and the opening words of *Improvement: Don Leaves Linda* will be: "To continue."

Music Word Fire and I Would Do It Again (Coo Coo)

A spin-off piece from *Perfect Lives* forms the basis of one of Ashley's most endearing recordings, released on vinyl by Lovely Music in 1981. While working on the opera Ashley received a fellowship from WNET television to make a one-episode pilot for the video of *Perfect Lives*. He didn't, however, want to create a single episode out of context, so instead he and John Sanborn fashioned a twenty-eight-minute pilot video that would represent the lessons from the bar scene, that is, the videotape that Baby watches to teach her to play boogie-woogie. These lessons merge with the pop song from the bank scene, and the piece is titled *Music Word Fire and I Would Do It Again (Coo Coo)*. The bar scene refers to "Thirty lessons guaranteed to merge / The left hand with the right," but these thirty get squeezed down for TV purposes to 28 one-minute variations in four groups of seven. Movement 1 (variations 1–7) is based on Isolde and centers around Kroesen intoning the bank song; movement 2, "Raoul de Noget," contains quotes from the *Perfect Lives* text read by Ashley; movement 3, "Buddy," is marked by repetitively static figurations played on prepared piano by Tyranny; and movement 4, "The Captain of the Football Team," emphasizes van Tieghem's electronic percussion.

Ashley, Tyranny, and Peter Gordon made the variations on the song by playing tapes over and over and improvising on them; afterward Ashley told the other two to choose the variations they thought were most successful. Sanborn and his then-frequent collaborator, video artist Kit Fitzgerald, developed a video for the piece, condensing the images of the entire opera into a twenty-eight-minute synopsis.[18] Sparse with regard to words, infectiously rhythmic, propelled by Gordon's boppy beat, and neither text- nor plot-driven, *Music Word Fire* is the closest thing Ashley has ever produced to a pop record. I have often used this piece to introduce newcomers and skeptics to his music, with excellent results. As of this writing, though, the work has regrettably not yet been reissued on compact disc.

6 Who Could Speak If Every Word Had Meaning?

Atalanta (Acts of God)

WHILE ASHLEY WAS AT MILLS COLLEGE, he would frequent a series of concerts in Berkeley by a group called the Arch Ensemble, run by Thomas Buckner. Buckner (b. 1941) was a New Yorker from a well-to-do family who had gone to Yale and, at nineteen, "run away from home" to San Francisco, where he worked at a factory and supported himself on the minimum wage. There he enrolled at the Jesuit University of Santa Clara, majoring in English, though from an early age he had always wanted to sing. Majoring in linguistics in graduate school at Stanford, he met David Wessel, a mathematical psychologist who would later be tapped by Pierre Boulez to help found his electronic music institute in Paris, IRCAM, by virtue of his groundbreaking work on computer-generated sound. With Wessel and composer-accordionist Pauline Oliveros, Buckner began improvising in 1965, and, starting in 1967, studied Indian vocal technique for a few years with the great Ali Akbar Khan (1922–2009) at the American Society for Eastern Arts. Buckner finally realized that linguistics was not his world and switched to a career in music.

Concertizing in the Berkeley area, Buckner decided he could run a better performance space than the ones available, so in 1972 he started 1750 Arch, a venue named for its address, to present early music, classical music, jazz, world music (not yet known by that term at the time), and new music. The space soon gave birth to an eponymous record label that was an important new-music source in the late 1970s and early 1980s (offering, among other things, the first recordings of the Nancarrow player piano studies). Buckner branched out still further by creating the 1750 Arch Ensemble, a twenty-three-member group that included most orchestral instruments, percussion, and electronics. The ensemble made it a point to commission local composers.[1]

Buckner remembers Ashley performing *The Wolfman* in an early concert (though the gig is missing on Ashley's list of performances). When the ensemble received a consortium grant in 1983, Buckner asked Ashley to write a piece for them, and he wanted to be included as a singer. Ashley wrote for him a chamber-orchestra version of something he was working on, the "Odalisque" song from a new opera, *Atalanta (Acts of God)* (1982–87). About this time Buckner moved back to New York City to have more opportunities to sing music by new composers, and he and Ashley worked together every afternoon. Buckner used his improvisational skills to find ways to sing Ashley's lines within Ashley's harmonies, and Ashley accommodated him by taking a more modal approach—no great stretch, given Ashley's early experience with jazz. Ashley was so happy with "Odalisque" that he admitted to Buckner that he was "trying him out." As a result, Buckner became a permanent member of Ashley's ensemble and introduced into *Atalanta* a singing style that brought the techniques of *Perfect Lives* into new territory.

Another singer who joined Ashley's permanent cast at this point was Jacqueline Humbert (b. 1952). At art school in Ann Arbor, she started out working with Ashley's filmmaker friend George Manupelli, went to York University, and at the latter school met the composer David Rosenboom, whom she married. The couple met Ashley at Mills, and Mary Ashley recommended that Humbert do the costume and makeup work for *Perfect Lives*, which she did, quite imaginatively. From 1976 to 1978 Humbert was also performing as a kind of avant-garde cabaret singer under the name J. Jasmine. At some point Ashley realized that she would be perfect for singing as well as costumes, and he asked her to be the Odalisque in *Atalanta* and Linda in *Improvement*. He particularly appreciated the fact that since she was from Detroit, she could imitate his speech patterns precisely. Humbert doesn't read music, and neither does Sam Ashley, but both exhibit a preternatural ability for memorizing and aural learning. From *Atalanta* on, Humbert brought a lithe and engaging new sensibility to Ashley's vocal writing.

Ashley and Mimi's Tribeca condominium is across the street from the Atalanta building, built in 1924, which used to be occupied by a food-importing company. Until 2000, when it was converted ("artistically destroyed," Ashley says) to condominiums, the word ATALANTA was painted in large letters across the side. Ashley started wanting to write an opera called *Atalanta* and learned from friends that the word was the name of a character from ancient Greek mythology who, abandoned by her royal father because she is a girl, is raised by animals. As a result she becomes legendarily strong, the fastest-running human. Her father takes her back to marry her off and increase his kingdom, but she imposes the condition that she will only marry someone who can outrun her. Those who compete and fail she kills with her spear.[2] But the clever Hippomenes, who loves her, consults Aphrodite, who gives him three golden apples to throw in front of Atalanta during the race. Stopping to pick them up, Atalanta loses the race. Aphrodite, however, tricked in the process by another goddess, retaliates by turning Atalanta and Hippomenes into leopards according to the ancient belief that leopards could not reproduce. Thus a recurring refrain in Ashley's opera about Atalanta is

> THE LEOPARD HAS
> SANCTUARY
> FAMILY TIES
> REPUTATION
> And in the leopard there is no beginning.

In Ashley's idiosyncratic cosmology, the three golden apples thrown in front of Atalanta are transformed into three characters: the great jazz pianist Bud Powell; Ashley's uncle Willard Reynolds, described by Ashley as a shaman or storyteller; and the surrealist painter (and Mimi's late uncle) Max Ernst. Max, Willard, and Bud represent three aspects of opera: image, narrative, and music. To make things more complicated, these three men were present during the bank robbery of *Perfect Lives*, mistaken by three of the tellers as possible suspects for the robbery. A spacecraft run by scientists arrives overhead at that moment; they are looking for the Atalanta race, but they have miscalculated their time by eight thousand years and beam up Max, Willard, and Bud by mistake.

Remember that in Ashley's historical scheme *Atalanta* precedes *Perfect Lives*, though it was written second. It deals with architecture (East Coast) as *Perfect Lives* was about agriculture (Midwest). *Atalanta* represents the European roots of American immigrants, and rather than isolated sayings (as in *Perfect Lives*), it is structured in anecdotes, which betray some consciousness of where one has come from.

Atalanta is actually three operas (the subtitle is "Three Operas by Robert Ashley"), one each for Max, Willard, and Bud. For purposes of the plot, the Odalisque is Atalanta centuries later, confined in her harem, the *oda*, and surrounded by her suitors. Each of the operas contains nine scenes, though only three of these are included in any one performance. Of the nine scenes two are paired in each opera and must be played together as one long scene: The "Character Reference" and the "Anecdote with Admonition and Song." The "Character Reference," in the voice of a narrator, is an introduction of the male "hero" of the opera: Max, Willard, or Bud. The "Anecdote with Admonition and Song" is an argument sung by the hero to the Odalisque (as the modern version of Atalanta) for the purpose of entertaining her. In the anecdote the hero is "showing off," and he is interrupted periodically by an admonition (for example, in Max, "You ought to be an employee of the state") to stop the showing off. The admonition is countered by a love song (by the hero) saying how he feels about his chances in his relationship with the "excellent woman."

The other seven scenes are interchangeable, and so a performance can be made of one of the paired scenes and any combination of the other seven scenes from any of the operas. The interchangeable scenes—"It's a Girl," "Odalisque," "Headlines," "Family Stories," "Gossip," "Problems in the Flying Saucer"—have different texts for each opera and may be used or not used. In addition, in each opera there is a long scene that doesn't have a generic title: "The Etchings" (Max), "Empire" (Willard), and "Au Pair" (Bud). The long scene can occur at any place in the sequence of scenes (except between "Character Reference" and "Anecdote.") So, from the many possible combinations of scenes, a different opera can be played every night. Ashley's notion was that this opera should have a mythical quality, since the tale of Atalanta is a myth.

Atalanta is the most ambitious and most complex of Ashley's texts and the most challenging to describe adequately; the entire text was published as a book in 2011 by Burning Books. In developing the opera, Ashley performed the core scenes, "Character Reference" and "Anecdote with Admonition and Song," with "Blue" Gene Tyranny (in a concert version designed by Lawrence Brickman and Paul Shorr), first in New York as part of the Lovely Music Live Festival in January 1982, then at the Pompidou Center in Paris at the Festival d'Automne, November 5–15, 1982, and subsequently in Cambridge, Massachusetts; Minneapolis; Madison; Fort Worth; and Philadelphia. The full opera, with added performers Sam Ashley, Jacqueline Humbert, and Thomas Buckner and with stage designer Lawrence Brickman and sound designer Paul Shorr, was premiered in Rome in 1983 and played subsequently in San Francisco, Chicago, Graz, Strasbourg, Vienna, Madrid, St. Louis, and London in the next five years.

So much of the original music for *Atalanta* was determined by "Blue" Gene Tyranny that it is best to describe his contribution in Ashley's own words:

"Blue" and I had an ongoing disagreement about the name of what I asked him to do. He called it "improvisation." I maintained that improvisation was different from what I was asking for. I wanted to call it "invention," because he had to make up his part, from no experience of what to expect, every time we performed. And this was because what everybody else in the ensemble would be doing at a particular moment was totally unpredictable. We never agreed. I don't care. He was consistently spectacular.[3]

The two recordings of *Atalanta* that Lovely Music has issued, separated by twenty-five years, provide the clearest possible example (though paralleled by the two recordings of *Perfect Lives*) of how much Ashley's works can differ from production to production, and also of how his musical proclivities have changed over the years. *Atalanta I* (to so designate the 1985 recording) is the loosest, freest, and most chaotic sounding disc of any Ashley opera. It was taken from a live performance at the Teatro Olimpico in Rome on March 9, 1985, for which most of the text was translated into Italian; in general, the odalisque and character reference scenes are mostly in Italian, the anecdotes mostly in English. For English speakers this poses an obstacle in familiarizing oneself with the text, but Ashley's theory of language as music admits of no such difficulty: "[A]ll of us, I believe, are thrilled to listen to a foreign language when we have no obligation to respond. Foreign language overheard is heard as music, in a way that we can never hear the language we speak. So, it is not musically crucial that we understand the words in operas in foreign languages."[4]

Atalanta I contains an entire performance of all three acts; *Atalanta II* (released in 2010) contains the three long scenes: "The Etchings" (Max), "Empire" (Willard), and "Au Pair" (Bud). The acts in *Atalanta I* begin with Max, then proceed to Willard, and then Bud, and each consists of "Odalisque," "Character Reference," and "Anecdote." The harmonic basis of the opera (which, like *Perfect Lives*, runs at a tempo of 72 beats per minute throughout) is a simple progression of six chords: B♭, A♭, G (sometimes G7), C7, E♭, G minor, most evident in the anecdotes. In the accompaniments to the odalisque and character reference sections, Tyranny improvises around (or in Ashley's words "invents upon") the chorales from the anecdote sections. For instance, if you listen to the first chorale in the Bud anecdote (2:27–2:57 in *Atalanta I*), you'll hear the melody and chords Tyranny had played in the Bud odalisque at 9:00 (the interlude) and again starting at 12:57.

Each anecdote scene is divided into eight two-and-a-half-minute units and concludes in a thirty-second chorale; the chorales altogether constitute a "love song" associated with that character. The background for each two-and-a-half-minute unit runs through the six chords, though with many variations as improvised by Tyranny. Often the final chord is omitted; sometimes Tyranny remains on the B♭ tonality (or G minor) throughout; some passages are purely rhythmic, based on the same harmony pattern, but with the harmonies *tacet*, as determined by Tyranny. In the Bud movement in *Atalanta I*, the chords are represented by a drone pitch on the root, sometimes alternating with the half-step above. A characteristic melody beginning with a motive D–D–E♭–F may run through each such section; it is audible here mostly in the Max anecdotes. The "Odalisques" and "Character References" are accompanied by improvisations based on the chorales of the love songs.

By great contrast, musical aspects of the *Atalanta II* recording are almost minimalist in their consistency. Here there are no live performers except for the vocalists; the "electronic orchestras" were created by Ashley and the composer he later came to rely on for electronics, Tom Hamilton. "The Etchings" runs through the six chords once, approximately five minutes per chord (chord changes coming at 5:06, 10:20, 17:14, 21:14, and 24:40), as various recurring melodies dot the landscape. "Empire" runs through the six chords twice, expressed in a syncopated six-beat ostinato in the following proportions:

	B♭	A♭	G7	C7	E♭	g
Time:	0:00	3:12	5:20	6:56	13:20	16:32
Measures:	48	32	24	96	48	48
	19:44	22:56	25:36	28:48	32:00	33:04
	48	40	48	48	16	80

"Au Pair," however, disregards this progression and is entirely in the key of E♭, the nine scenes set off by ostinatos with different rhythms. Here Ashley uses the unusual device of both unifying the set and differentiating the scenes by associating each with a motive of two rising half-steps:

Lewis	F–G♭–G
Gretchen	A♭–A–B♭ (used within a longer melody)
Ingrid	B♭–B–C
Andrea	D♭–D–E♭
Leisel	E♭–E–F
Simone	F–G♭–G (embedded within a longer melody)
Katja	A♭–A–B♭ (in the bass)
Justine	B♭–B–C (embedded within the ostinato)
Lili Marlena	B♭–B–C
Epilogue	E♭–E–F

Note that until "Lili Marlena" the motives ascend through a chromatic scale from scene to scene.

Atalanta I allows the singers considerable freedom in their pacing. Several voices are heard in free counterpoint; Buckner sings the text that Ashley is simultaneously speaking, so there is much echoing of phrases, while singers Carla Tatò and Jacqueline Humbert sing "headline" phrases in Italian. In *Atalanta II*, the text flows between Humbert and Ashley in rhythmic unisons that clearly took much rehearsal to coordinate. Overall, *Atalanta I* harks back to Ashley's attempts in compositions for the ONCE Group to create a musical space in which performers could take liberties. *Atalanta II* is stylistically closer to late works such as *Your Money My Life Goodbye*, *Foreign Experiences*, and *Now Eleanor's Idea*, in which voices fuse, momentum is inexorable, and rhythms are predetermined in rehearsal. Between these two extremes, one could imagine many other performance possibilities.

The opening odalisque, with the text Ashley originally set for Buckner, talks around the Atalanta story:

Imagine this:
A woman is known to excel above all others.
She even excels among men.
YOU SAY TO YOURSELF, SILENTLY, HOW IS THAT POSSIBLE.
Thus, the beginning is less than propitious.
We are fascinated with the idea of achievement.[5]

The character references and anecdotes are sometimes stories, at other times circuitous and revealing explanations of Ashley's theories about music and speech, such as this Max anecdote from *Atalanta I* (the Sargasso Sea reference is a partial quotation from the Ezra Pound poem *Portrait d'Une Femme*):

For instance, when we are young and among the young ones and need to be taught,
first lesson is that speech is different from—unh—meaning.
Otherwise, it would be impossible.
Who could speak, if every word had meaning? . . .
Right beneath the brain there is a thing we call the throat, and you can teach it to do anything.
It's one of the great ones.
One of the things is what we call vibration.
Now, vibration feels good, you know.
And, do you know why?
It's because in that most precious part of us, the brain, we are all connected.
You heard me. We are all connected.
We are connected, each one of us to all of us.
And that is the source of our suffering. Get back, worms.

We are connected, or there would be no more of us.
It would be vast and empty, and the beaches would stare back at the stars, and there might be other things, but there would be no more of us.
Exit us, if there were no connections. . . .
So, to protect those connections, which are our Sargasso Sea—(Boy, that's a hard one. You are our Sargasso Sea. Nice going, man.)
—we have to talk to slow things down.
I mean, the connections would blow up, if we did not have talk to slow things down.
Or, think of it this way: If we did not have talk, or vibrations from the throat, the brain would just sit there like a lump of pudding, looking only, and gradually the connections would just waste away. (22–23)

The Bud character reference in *Atalanta I* (heard only in Italian on the recording) sounds like Ashley having a philosophical conversation with himself about the purpose of music:

> I said, "Is the struggle with the law manifested in every aspect of the making of music, or are there law-abiding aspects and others that are confrontational only because of indiscretion on the musician's part—because of a transgression?"
>
> He said to me, "Music is the enactment of the manifestation of the struggle with the law on a scale of continuous attempts; that is, where the attempts are related to each other symbolically through a pattern imposed on our memory. Music is a history of our struggle with the law."
>
> I said, "Can music, then, substitute itself for the enactment of the struggle in other parts of our lives?"
>
> He said to me, "That is its most common use."
>
> I said, "The musician, then, becomes socially symbolic, enacting restlessness."
>
> He said to me, "Yes. In order to be law-abiding, there has to be a place where one can rest. One can be law-abiding only in safety from the law."
>
> I said, "Is the listener different from the musician?"
>
> He said to me, "Yes, that is the paradox of music. In listening to music we are observing other persons like ourselves, but the consequences of their actions do not accrue to us actually. Their actions are understood only in retrospect. The consequences may accrue to us as wisdom. May even endanger our relationship to the law, may change our minds, but for the listener the act has already come into existence before the law is recognized. The listener is in safety from the law." (120–21)

And another anecdote from Bud (not heard on either recording) seems to indicate something about the contrast between speech and music, between the right-brain enjoyment of sound for its own sake and the left-brain perception of meaningful content:

Take a word. It accumulates an image. Go as quick as possible to the next word.
A little moving picture show.
Here comes politics.
Right after the recent craze for freedom—
He's talking about a hundred and fifty years ago—
came the problem of how fast to go.
He's talking about moving through the story.
It started slow. The way it did in the old country. Notice that slow is slow. When it starts to mean something, we crave fast. When slow starts to mean something, we crave fast.
Let that be a lesson to you. (134)

Atalanta II is made entirely for the voices of Ashley and Humbert, either in dialogue or, in "Empire," overlapping on unison phrases. "The Etchings" is a close description of two images from Max Ernst's 1934 collage-novel *Une Semaine de Bonté* (A Week of Kindness), which combines images from Victorian novels to create a dark, surrealistic world of bird-people and violated women. The description fuses two images: a man getting out his wallet to show a police officer and going through its mundane contents in detail and a man seducing a woman police officer. "Au Pair" is a text written by Jacqueline Humbert based on her embroidered experiences with au pair girls. This story is pure comedy. In mock amazement Humbert tells her tales of au pairs molesting children, eating compulsively, having sex, and taking drugs as Ashley, tongue firmly in cheek, pretends to be scandalized. (When a Swedish au pair calls a child "Liddle coox-ooker," Ashley wryly speculates, "Swedish for something.") While the story has no direct relevance to Bud Powell, the great bebop pianist whose opera it belongs to, Ashley wanted to refer obliquely to the disjunction of the black-white experience and found this a solution: "the au pairs have one idea about what is going on and their employers have another."[6]

"Empire" is one of Ashley's most magnificent texts, and one he has often performed separately as a reading, without musical background. It is a Depression-era story about Ashley staying with his grandmother and seeing her feed the "extra men," that is, the unmarried men who went out on the road and became hobos or beggars. Some of the following phrases become a repeated refrain:

My grandmother would open the back door without fear. That seems like a strange thing to say now. The extra man would offer to help around the house, meaning in the yard or in the garage. My grandmother would say that that was not necessary. She would ask him to sit on the back steps and wait.

> Then she would close the door and cook. She made two eggs with bacon and fried potatoes. Two cups of coffee and two pieces of toast. If there was a pie from the night before, which was always, my grandmother would add a piece of pie. Everything was on one plate, except for the pie. The pie was on a separate plate. (100)

From this reminiscence, all the more touchingly drawn for its objectivity, Ashley moves into the Depression-era strategy of going into a restaurant, ordering a cup of hot water (which was free), pouring oneself a little catsup (also free), and making tomato soup. As his mental camera continues to pan outward from the domestic to the corporate, he moves into a larger story of Heinz beating Campbell in the catsup market ("Heinz fell into a torpor of success. Fifty-seven things and they all taste alike"), and then Campbell inventing canned tomato soup to take over another part of the market. This crescendoing saga of corporate growth brought about pervasive changes in society:

> My grandmother put a lock on her door. In case the Japs came. Everybody worked in factories. Former extra men all over day-dreamed. The roads were closed. Yards watched by g-men. My aunt stopped making pies. They went uneaten. Movies about Pacific islands. Really boring. Everybody wanted whatever could be canned. For the first time the banks owned the water. . . .
>
> . . . The Russians will drink Coca-Cola. The Chinese Pepsi. Or is it the other way around? Thank god for a corporate world divided. Thank god for tomato soup over Catholics or French . . .
>
> Look at the world. This is where we live. Some guy says now that in twenty years or so, Europeans will forget what summer was. Does that answer your question? (108–9)

Ashley says the story is true, but he had changed the food products to protect the "innocent."

7 If You Have to Ask You Can't Afford One

Now Eleanor's Idea

THE FIVE-AND-A-HALF-HOUR TETRALOGY *Now Eleanor's Idea* (1985–94) represents the conclusion of the American adventure, of Ashley's "history of our consciousness as Americans." If *Atalanta* represented the life of European immigrants in the eastern United States, remembering stories about the old country, and *Perfect Lives* the life in the Midwest, preserved in sayings whose origins are murky, *Now Eleanor's Idea*, with its four symmetrical parts, represents the great coming together in the Los Angeles of the future, with fragmented identities that need to be reconstituted. The tetralogy could be called Ashley's magnum opus, a mammoth continuum. Its operas—*Improvement: Don Leaves Linda*, *eL/Aficionado*, *Foreign Experiences*, and (the "title opera") *Now Eleanor's Idea*—are clearly differentiated by style and density.

The fact of a tetralogy owes at least something to the stable of four singers that Ashley had put together, and each opera capitalizes on a different voice, representing a character originally from *Perfect Lives*:

Improvement	Jacqueline Humbert	Linda (one of the bank tellers)
eL/Aficionado	Thomas Buckner	Don Jr. (D, captain of the football team)
Foreign Experiences	Sam Ashley	Junior Jr. (Don and Linda's son)
Now Eleanor's Idea	Joan La Barbara	Now Eleanor (another teller)

(Additional characters also appear—a doctor and Mr. Payne in *Improvement*, interrogators in *eL/Aficionado*, and so on.) Nominally, all four operas are couched in a key signature of four flats (F minor), although the twenty-four-note row of *Improvement* and the bebop chords of the other three operas include plenty of accidentals. Broad areas of symmetry operate across the tetralogy, as can be seen from a comparison of durations and tempos (see table 1).

TABLE 1. Duration and tempo in the four operas of *Now Eleanor's Idea*

Opera	Duration in minutes	Tempo	Duration in beats
Improvement	88:05	♩= 72	6,336 ♩
eL/Aficionado	71:43	♩= 72	not all measured
Foreign Experiences	72:20	♩= 90	6,336 ♩
Now Eleanor's Idea	88:28	♩= 72	6,336 ♩

The outer operas are each eighty-eight minutes long, the middle two operas seventy-two minutes each. All are at a tempo of 72 bpm except *Foreign Experiences*, at a faster 90 bpm. Three of the operas are the same length in quarter notes, 6,336; *Improvement*'s two acts divide that length in half (3,168 + 3,168), and the last two operas divide it into four equal acts of 1,584 beats each. Clearly this is not coincidence. In fact, the original plan was to make all the operas the same length and structure.[1] The fact that *eL/Aficionado* doesn't quite fit the pattern may be because it wasn't originally conceived as part of this work. The remaining opera was originally meant to be titled "When Opportunity Knocks," and *eL/Aficionado*, having grown out of a solo piece for Tom Buckner named *My Brother Called*, seemed to Ashley an acceptable substitute.

Figure 3 reveals more aspects of symmetry among the four works. Act 1 of *Improvement* is in 3/4, and act 2 is in 4/4. In *Foreign Experiences*, the outer acts are in 4/4 and the middle acts in 3/4. *Now Eleanor's Idea* is the opposite, except that the mostly 4/4 middle acts have intros and endings in 3/4. *Improvement* and *eL/Aficionado* are both composed of scenes of irregular length, the two remaining operas in four acts of identical length.

Is it important for the listener to know about these symmetries of proportion among Ashley's work? I think on one level it is; at least, while listening to the endless and initially confusing outpouring of Ashley's text, it is worth cultivating a sense that his is ultimately an ordered universe, so that one can learn to perceive the large-scale balance behind the sometimes apparent chaos. Ashley's operas emulate the "theater of memory" of the Renaissance occult thinker Gior-

Improvement: Don Leaves Linda

Scene:	Pre	1	2	3	4	5	6	7	8	9	10	11	12	13	14	15	16	17	18	19	20	21	22	23
Mm.:	36	31	38	63	165	38	108	49	54	249	90	99	36	83	148	109	56	56	157	96	32	9	30	16

1056 mm. of 3 = 3168 ♩ — 792 mm. of 4 = 3168 ♩

6336 ♩

eL/Aficionado

Scene	1	2	3	4	5	6	7	8	9	10
Mm.	96mm of 3 288 ♩	324 ♩	324 ♩	204mm. of 6 1224 ♩	324 ♩	324 ♩	432mm. of 3 1296 ♩	288 ♩	488 ♩	306 ♩

5186 ♩

Foreign Experiences

Act I	Act II	Act III	Act IV
396 mm. of 4	528 mm. of 3	528 mm. of 3	396 mm. of 4
1584 ♩	1584 ♩	1584 ♩	1584 ♩

6336 ♩

Now Eleanor's Idea

Act I	Act II	Act III	Act IV
528 mm. of 3	72 mm. of 3 = 216	72 mm. of 3 = 216	528 lines x 3
1584 ♩	324 mm. of 4 = 1296	288 mm. of 4 = 1152	1584 ♩
	24 mm. of 3 = 72	72 mm. of 3 = 216	
	1584 ♩	1584 ♩	

6336 ♩

FIGURE 3. Symmetry among four Ashley works

dano Bruno, in that an orderly, symmetrical structure is created to house all of the heterogeneous materials collected in them. Alternatively, one might read Hans T. David writing about the sonata from Bach's *Musical Offering*:

> The sonata reflects the form of the whole work in a remarkable manner. The first movement is long-drawn-out, the third and fourth being shorter, so that in performance the first takes as long as the other two together. The result is that the quick second movement appears as the center of the piece, which also means that it is also the center of the whole work. . . . This movement, a long Allegro, is in five sections, like the whole in the midst of which it lies. The second section uses the same materials as the first in somewhat altered sequence and order of modulations. . . . The middle part B, slightly longer than the other parts, is again symmetrical in its use of materials.[2]

It is certainly tempting to think that Bach's obsessive concern for symmetry and proportion, imparted to Ashley by David, the leading Bach scholar of his teachers' generation, gave Ashley a respect for such principles that shaped his own work.

With the *Now Eleanor's Idea* operas, two more permanent members entered Ashley's ensemble: singer Joan La Barbara (b. 1947) and recording engineer Tom Hamilton (b. 1946). A virtuoso of avant-garde voice and a composer of electronic and chamber works herself, La Barbara has had an extensive career outside Ashley's works. She sang with Steve Reich from 1971 to 1974 and later worked with Glass, and Lucier and Behrman had written works for her in the Sonic Arts Union days, when Ashley met her. She taught at CalArts from 1980 to 1985, and in 1989 Ashley called her to involve her in *Improvement*; as Now Eleanor, she has had a major role in every work since. Hamilton, like Ashley, had both directed an academic electronic studio and made commercial soundtracks. Moving to New York in 1987, he instinctively understood Ashley's aims and became indispensable as someone who could make the technology happen.[3]

Improvement: Don Leaves Linda

Improvement: Don Leaves Linda is Ashley's most elaborately constructed opera, and in that sense his most ambitious before *Quicksand*. It takes the form of allegory. Ashley, as narrator, begins the opera by explaining what Now Eleanor's idea is: that the major religions in America—Judaism, Protestantism, Modernism, Science, Theater (and elsewhere in the text Business is added)—have merged and become one, their differences evaporated. Then, more quickly, he says, "For the sake of argument, Don is Spain in 1492, and Linda is the Jews." And we're off. In Spain in 1492 the monarchs, Isabella I of Castile and Ferdinand II of Aragon, issued the Alhambra Decree, giving Jews four months to leave the country. Ashley's idea is that half of that Spanish energy went to Italy and thence into the East Coast of the Unites States, half to Latin America directly, and that they meet up, at the end of the tetralogy, in Los Angeles.

The music for *Improvement* is the most minutely structured that Ashley has ever used in an opera. There are 23 scenes plus a prelude, 12 scenes and the prelude in the first act, 11 scenes in the second. The harmony shifts back and forth between B♭ minor and F minor. For instance, scene 1 is over an F harmony; scene 2 has 18 measures on B♭, followed by 18 on F; Scene 3 has 9 measures on B♭, 18 on F, 18 on B♭, 18 on F; the long fourth scene is entirely on B♭; and so on. The piece is based on a row of 24 pitches containing every note of the chromatic scale except D:

Act 1	Act 2
F–G–C–G–B𝄫–A♭–E♭–B♭–C–D♭–E♭–F–G	G–C–F♭–C♭–B♭–B♭–F–F♯–G–A♭–F

Because of this, Ashley likes to refer to it as a passacaglia, a seventeenth-century form of variations over a repeating ground bass. Each pitch corresponds to one scene, including the prelude. Each scene introduces the new pitch, which is the main reciting pitch for the main character of that scene. Secondary voices sing pitches held over from previous scenes or occasionally anticipating the next scene. Thus the vocal pitches on which the characters chant proceed as given in table 2. More singable secondary melodies are formed when needed for choral transitions by linking segments of the row. Some of these segments run repetitively through the background of scenes.

TABLE 2. Vocal pitches in *Improvement*

Prelude:	Narrator:	**F**				
1.	Chorus	**G**				
2.	Carla	**C**	Carlo	G		
3.	Don + Chorus	**G**				
4.	M1 + M2	**B♭♭**	F1	G	F2	C
5.	Carlo	**A♭**	Carla	B♭♭		
6.	Linda	**E♭**				
7.	Linda	**B♭**	Chorus	A♭		
8.	Linda	**C**	Chorus	F	Mr. Payne	F
9.	Linda	**D♭**	Mr. Payne	C	Chorus	F
10.	Mrs. Payne.	**E♭**	Linda	D♭	Chorus	F
11.	Jr., Jr.	**F**	Chorus	D♭	Mr. Payne	C
12.	Narr. + Linda	**G**				
13.	Narrator	**G**	Chorus	C	Melody	
14.	Linda	**C**	Doctor	G		
15.	Linda	**F♭**	Narrator	C♭	C	G
16.	Narrator	**C♭**				
17.	Narrator	**B♭**	Doctor	B♭	Mrs. Payne	B♭
18.	Linda	**B♭**	Narrator	F		
19.	Linda	**F**	Jr., Jr.	F		
20.	Linda	**F♯**	Chorus	C		
21.	Melody (mostly **G** and C)					
22.	Linda	**A♭**	Chorus	G		
23.	Linda	**F**	Chorus	A♭		

In addition to Don's being Spain and Linda's being the Jews, there are many other historical correspondences in Ashley's allegory. George Payne, who takes an interest in Linda, is Giordano Bruno, who based much of his work on the Jewish Kabbalah. Payne's mother represents the Catholic Church. Tap dancing, a specialty of Payne's, is Bruno's *Art of Memory*. Left-handed golf, which Junior Jr. tries to learn, is cosmology. The airline ticket counter is the Spanish Inquisition.

Don's dramatic leaving of Linda opens the story. On a car trip to the Southwest, he simply drives off and leaves her in the restroom at a roadside rest stop, heading for the airport alone. Linda will be given a ride by strangers. At the airport ticket counter, Don and Linda take the names Carlo and Carla; she is his inquisitor as, later, he becomes hers. An otherworldly quality is imparted by the fact that each answer is given before the question is finished, alternating lines sung at the same time, as though this is a ritual of which both parties know the outcome:

Do you have a ticket?
    Yes.
The ticket says that it was issued as one of two.
    Yes.
The ticket says that you came here with your wife.
    Yes.
Where is your wife?
    She is not here.
Why is she not here?
    She stayed behind.
Ordinarily we would not honor such a ticket.
    I understand.
But today is a special day.
    I know . . .
Why did she stay behind?
    I left her behind.
Why did you leave her behind?
    I had to leave urgently.
What is the reason for such urgency?
    My reasons are my own.
Do you refuse to tell me the reason?
    No.
What is the reason?
    Another person.
Is that person a woman?
    Yes. . . .

Your wife will be angry and jealous.
No.
How is that possible?[4]

The questions come in languid periods of three beats each, like a slow, listless waltz. Don's lengthy and hastily delivered answer to the final question constitutes Scene 3, "The Correspondences Text," identified in the allegory as "Exploration," meaning the Spanish exploration of the New World. Don converses somewhat vaguely on the significance of great works of architecture throughout history: the ziggurats at Ur, the pyramids at Giza, the World Trade Center, and when he finishes, asking, "Do you know what I mean?" Linda answers for many of us: "Well, sort of. I get the idea that this is a subject that you are interested in."

Linda finds herself being picked up and driven to the airport by the Unimportant Family ("Four people too much alike. / A typical trap. She accepts."). Once at the airport, she undergoes a set of questions parallel to those of scene 3, and in answer to the last, explains (in scene 6, "The Indifference Text") why she is not angry and jealous:

My husband
is embarked upon an adventure of the mind—
if I may use that word. Inevitably,
his partner in the adventure would be another woman—
to address the question that is most troubling to you—
else the adventure would not be, precisely, "of the
mind." He has gone to determine if there is
continuance apart from the continuance of things. . . .

. . . That that moment—the moment of
crossing the threshold—should come in a form
that seems dramatic to you, that
it should come while I am at a toilet in
the middle of a desert, is more acceptable to me,
more generous on his part, more friendly,
because it is clearer and, thus, more humorous,
more human than had it come hidden, ambiguous,
timid and without confidence in me.
He would never go out after dinner to buy a pack of
cigarettes and not return. His imagination is
bigger than that.[5]

The other woman, of course, is Eleanor, representing America: in the mythology, America, or rather, the Americas, where the Spanish went exploring.

On the flight home Linda meets Mr. Payne, who represents Giordano Bruno (1548–1600). Bruno was an Italian philosopher, astronomer, and mathematician who was burned at the stake at the Campo dei Fiori in Rome for his heretical views. He was pursued as a heretic for questioning the divinity of Christ, for reading books that the church had put on the index, and also possibly for positing a heliocentric view of the universe, which he regarded as infinite and possibly containing other, similar worlds. He devoted much work to a system he called "the art of memory," which in Ashley's cosmology becomes tap dancing. Linda recounts the humiliating experience of dropping her purse at the airline ticket counter and having the contents spill out. She realizes in retrospect that Mr. Payne has memorized the contents, and when he courts her afterward, he says, "Let me guess what's in your purse. / For everything I get right I get a kiss."

Once home, Mr. Payne takes Linda and Junior Jr. to supper at his mother's house. Linda questions Mrs. Payne about why she considers pasta the perfect food and eats it at every meal. She replies that, at three hundred calories per cup (with sauce), "the importance of pasta is the importance of a standard," a predictable measurement. We move into the future for the next scene, and Junior Jr., now a successful businessman, reminisces about Mr. Payne's trying to teach him left-handed golf (Bruno's cosmology). The last word comes from Mr. Payne, informing us that his attempted romance with Linda didn't work out. "She danced away. . . . She likes loneliness. She will / spend her days in loneliness."

Act 2, as the chorus intones, "is about—uhn—public opinion" and the conflicts it causes for Linda (the Jews). The scene opens with Linda moving to the big city, symbolizing the urbanization of the Jews. The city is in turn represented by another of Ashley's pop songs, this one about Tarzan, its verses punctuated with the sampled wails of angry elephants:

Here come Tarzan.
  Look at that suntan.
He's a big swinger.

He got a wife an'
  Her name Jane an'
She's a humdinger. . . .

Hangin' around with the apes all day
What a way to raise a fa-mo-ly.

Staying on the radio for weeks, the song becomes popular but infects everyone with an air of disenchantment. The narrator says:

If it is not so good in
The world capital of civilization, where is it good?
Celebrities continue to die of disappointment.
The very poor continue to die of hunger.
The unrecognized continue to die of striving.

Scene 14 represents Freudian psychotherapy: Linda discusses a dream with a doctor (sung by Adam Klein, son of Howard Klein of the Rockefeller Foundation) who keeps interrupting her, usually with the words "Just a moment, please," and after each interruption Linda reflexively replies, "I'm sorry." The doctor's voice is made more portentous by being filtered through a harmonizer. In the dream, Linda is standing in a meadow, and a propeller plane flies over her from a great height. Someone calls Linda's name from the plane. Linda insists that the dream was surprising and natural and made her happy, while the doctor insists that her description expresses a subconscious feeling of foreboding. At last the doctor gives a rather pompous interpretation of the dream, actually a lecture on how the offering of images is a secularization of Judaism ("as Protestantism is a / Secularization of Christianity, Modernism is the secularization / of taste").

The next two scenes, "The Good Life" and "Trouble," are temporally intertwined—the music switches back and forth between them. In the first, Linda and a companion (Buckner) discuss nutrition in a restaurant, with many references to drugs (valium, cigarettes, marijuana, cocaine), but several drunken oafs in brown shirts at an adjoining table (standing for the Nazis) begin making fun of them. In a scene symbolizing the Holocaust, Linda and her companion try to leave, but two men grab her companion, who punches the worse offender in the face. Waiters assert their authority, and police arrive, signifying the necessity of military force. The final scenes, "A Place in the Country," "Happiness, Prosperity and Forgetfulness," and the ensuing bridge game, portray the emigration of Jews to Israel and a home of their own. Linda's successes in the city are punctuated by a refrain that she sings, doubtfully intertwining materialism and epistemology: "This is as high as I can go / How do you know that you know it?" (The apparent 3/8-meter groupings in this phrase makes an effective interruption of the prevailing sense of time.)

The remainder of the text is filled with references to Judaism, some historical, some personal only to Ashley. Linda "wins a large cash prize in the lottery"—this refers to Israel's achievement of self-determination in 1948. "She is trapped with a man in an elevator"—this is Albert Einstein, one of whose famous examples demonstrating relativity involved a man in a falling elevator observing a bullet shot through the elevator. In scene 18, lines bounce among Mr. Payne, his mother, Junior Jr., the doctor, and the narrator, as each of them echoes short phrases intoned first by the chorus. One by one Linda dismisses phases of her life with the phrase, "Oh well, forget it."

A personal subtext is that as Linda goes back in time toward Atlantis, at the end of the opera, she develops into a portrait of the woman who lived across Kimberley Road from Ashley's childhood Packard Road home, an exotic and "voluptuous" Russian Jewish woman named Monya Hariton, who liked to have friends over for bridge.[6] And so the opera ends in a bridge game. Linda reads a letter from Junior Jr., who has a new job at a factory that makes "a very common object that we never see"—this is a reference to the ball-bearing factory in *Atalanta*. Four brief last scenes are devoted to the four players in the bridge game, actually four locations. North is Berlin, where the Holocaust was masterminded but which is still linked with nostalgia. East is the River Rouge Ford plant in Dearborn, Michigan, which on its completion in 1928 was the world's largest factory. Its significance here within the history of the Jews (aside from being the place where Ashley's uncle Willard worked) is that Henry Ford was an admirer of Hitler and was awarded the Grand Cross of the German Eagle by the Nazis in July 1938.[7] This occasions a brief song about the biggest building in the world: "I don't care what you say / Words can never change it / Money talks."

South is the Campo dei Fiori in Rome, where Giordano Bruno was burned at the stake in 1600 and which is now graced with a statue of him. Here, Linda keeps singing about 28,278,466 people facing the same way and allowing their photo to be snapped, people who could possibly perish in a flash of light. The number 28,278,466 also happens to be the minimum number of people for whom version 6 of Ashley's *Public Opinion Descends upon the Demonstrators* could be performed, a number Ashley associates with the end of the world. Finally, West is Atlantis, the ancient island mentioned in Plato's *Critias*, which may have been the site of an ancient civilization that perished in an upheaval of the earth. Linda's final vision has encompassed everything from the origins of human history to the end of the world.

eL/Aficionado

One of Ashley's simplest works, musically as well as textually, *eL/Aficionado* is an opera derived from the language of personals ads, which became very popular in the 1980s. The piece started off as a smaller chamber piece titled *My Brother Called*, for Thomas Buckner on vocals, "Blue" Gene Tyranny on piano, and a soundtrack created on the Gulbransen Palace Organ, in which form it was performed several times from 1987 to 1990. Eventually Ashley expanded *My Brother Called* into *eL/Aficionado*, originally scoring it for two pianos (played by Tyranny and Joseph Kubera). This version was premiered April 14, 1988, in Marseille, France, presented by the Groupe de Musique Experimental de Marseille at the Theatre National de Marseille. Orchestrating the piece to fit smoothly into the tetralogy, which Ashley did three years afterward, required considerable rewriting.

As the "slow movement" of the tetralogy, *eL/Aficionado* is lyrical and lovely to listen to, but its text is tense and suspenseful, inspired by meticulous espionage techniques detailed in John Le Carré's novels. The conceit of the opera is that Buckner, the main soloist, is an agent in the "Department" who is answering the questions of interrogators (Ashley, Sam Ashley, and Jacqueline Humbert). The agent explains that he received a telephone call from his brother ("He is not my brother in the ordinary sense. / It is a word we use in the department. / It means someone you can count on")[8] instructing him to go to a nearby restaurant, where the waiter will tell him he has a phone call. The phone and the menu (which contains the code to describe the people going into the building) are brought to the table and, casually if conspicuously, the agent is to describe everyone entering the apartment building across the street using the code of personals ads.

Capitalizing on Buckner's jazz training, Ashley based the entire piece on a sequence of sixteen jazz chords, in four groups of four. Chords in each of the four groups all share the same melodic mode on which Buckner improvises his line:

Chords	1–4: D♭ major scale
"	5–8: C♭ major scale
"	9–12: D♭ rising melodic minor
"	13–16: A♭ major scale

Each group is also associated with four "starting notes" on which phrases on those chords should begin. Scenes 2, 3, 5, 6, 8, and 10 are all titled "My Brother Called." These scenes, plus scene 1, "Personal," are all either four minutes long, or four and a half, or in-between. In each of these scenes the chord changes come every fifteen seconds (18 beats at a tempo of 72 bpm), and Buckner sings a line over that chord. In the movements that are longer than four minutes, there is either a thirty-second introduction before the chords start, or in the case of the last movement, a brief dénouement. Within each four-chord group, each of the starting tones begins one of the four phrases. For instance, the starting notes for the first group are G♭, A♭, E♭, and C, so the first phrase always begins with G♭, and the other phrases are assigned the other starting notes in a permutational pattern different for each scene. Since the biggest harmonic changes come between the four-chord groups, the listener will notice a particular harmony (or key-) change at 1:00, 2:00, and 3:00 in the four-minute movements and at 1:30, 2:30, and 3:30 in the 4:30 movements.

The set of scenes titled "My Brother Called" is interrupted by three longer scenes, two of them flashbacks from the past. In "A Simple Border Crossing" the agent is asked to reconstruct his first assignment, which was to enter a strange building and memorize the labyrinthine order of rooms there—perhaps again an evocation of Bruno's theater of memory. This scene takes about seventeen minutes to go through the chord progression more slowly, over a low B♭ drone articulated every six beats (or five seconds). A background melody wanders chromatically between D♭ and the A♭ above it. Eight times during the dialogue, at irregular intervals, Ashley, as interrogator, incites a louder chorus section in voices speaking together, saying, "Recite Designed by Well-known Architect, please," or, "Recite Restored to Classic Elegance, please." These choruses are mostly descriptions of houses in the style of real estate ads, although two of them merely reiterate a phrase from *Perfect Lives*: "There is an absoluteness to surprise, he thinks," alluding to Raoul de Noget's musings about one's consciousness of death. ("Where does that come from?" the agent responds. "I read it somewhere.") "A Simple Border Crossing" is a rather abstract discussion of aspects of espionage; the actual labyrinth is described in the subsequent two "My Brother Called" scenes.

The second longer scene, "An Answer Is Expected," sends the agent to a safehouse where a child with occult powers is being held by a couple with a dog. The agent describes a house in the woods, a little reminiscent of the house in the first *Doctor Chicago* film. The boy, less than ten years old but very adult-acting, even arrogant, and with presumed occult powers, tells the agent that he will see a dog and that it will be terrifying. The agent first thinks this is the older couple's dog, but the terrifying dog, looking through a window, doesn't appear until the agent is about to leave.

> And it was terrifying. Like he had said.
> There was a coldness in the room.
> I hope I will never feel that feeling again.

Here the chords last either one minute (72 beats) or 90 seconds (108 beats), the longer chords accommodating interrogator 1's (Ashley's) lengthier comments. Key changes between chord groups come at 4:30, 9:00, and 14:00.

The penultimate scene, "Viva's Boy," is kind of a debriefing, a dialogue among the agent and his interrogators. The agent explains aspects of his code:

2ND INTERR.: It seems unlikely that something as peculiar as the reciting of a list of personals to a phone-caller would go unnoticed in a café.

THE AGENT: As I understood the assignment, my job was not to go unnoticed. As you must know, no arrangements can be perfect in this calling. Or, perhaps they were perfect. I did as I was told.

3RD INTERR.: There were too many words of different sorts for your explanation to be believable.

THE AGENT: It is not important to me that you believe me. You called me here. . . . Most of what happened makes no sense to me.

In "Viva's Boy" the chord changes every 23.3 seconds (28 beats at 72 bpm, though the beat is not articulated).

Foreign Experiences

Foreign Experiences may be one of Ashley's most difficult operas to approach, but it is a rewarding one. With its four symmetrical acts (1 and 4 high-energy, 2 and 3 lower-energy), each almost devoid of significant internal articulation, it denies the listener the memorable stand-out scenes or piquant moments of *Perfect Lives* or *Improvement* and equally the linear stories of *Atalanta* and *Dust*; it is truly an eventless work. Another barrier for some is its wealth of profanity, for here Ashley repeats and develops the idea from *Atalanta* that swearing slows down speech, making thought more possible:[9]

> Instead, I learn to swear. Fuck, how simple!
> It's so mother-fucking simple. You Swear.
> Instead of talking all the time, you swear.
> And since foul language fucks the tempo,
> The fucking thing slows down, and you start
> Thinking again! (59)

Yet the text overall is rich, dense with allusion, almost phantasmagorical at times, making so many references to Ashley's other works that it seems almost like a focal point in his output. The opera is a portrait of Ashley as he must have felt at Mills College, after his divorce and before he met Mimi Johnson. Even by Ashley's standards, this opera is strongly autobiographical, not only in the actions it portrays but in musical terms: Ashley's 1959 Piano Sonata runs through the background of act 1, a 1990 work titled *Yellow Man with Heart with Wings* runs through act 4, and texts from earlier Ashley works get wryly worked into the libretto itself.

One must understand *Foreign Experiences* against the background of a series of books that was sweeping America in the 1970s: the *Don Juan* books of the elusive and enigmatic Carlos Castaneda (1925?-98), an anthropologist whose descriptions of his alleged drug-fueled shamanistic experiences caught on like wildfire. As an anthropology student at UCLA, Castaneda claimed to have met a Yaqui Indian named Don Juan Matus who, through a combination of ancient wisdom and hallucinogenic substances, could manipulate space and time. Castaneda's first book, *The Teachings of Don Juan: A Yaqui Way of Knowledge*, appeared in 1968, followed by *A Separate Reality: Further Conversations with Don Juan* (1971) and *Journey to Ixtlan: The Lessons of Don Juan* (1972).[10] Although Castaneda's books were widely read, perfectly attuned as they were to the crescendoing 1970s interest in hallucinogenics, a wealth of critical doubt soon came to cause them to be regarded as works of fiction. In fact, the most critical commentary was brought out by Richard DeMille, whose wife was a friend of Mimi Johnson's aunt Dorothea Tanning, and with whom Ashley corresponded on the subject. *Foreign Experience*'s story of Don Jr. meeting an Indian guide on the Mexican border clearly harks back to Don Juan, though the deflated dénouement is almost comically different—perhaps even a cynical satire on Castaneda's fictional exploits.

The background story: Don Jr. has come, with Linda and Junior Jr. and a friend named N (Ashley's friend Nick Bertoni), to take a job at a small college in California, "from the Midwest of fractured identities to the world of no identities"[11]—just as Ashley himself left Ann Arbor for Mills College. On visiting the campus on a Sunday afternoon, they find it haunted by a well-documented evil ghost who frequents the building of Don Jr.'s office and the faculty village behind it. In the next few months Don Jr. goes mad and becomes irrational. Ashley's description of him is a self-portrait: "His family has disintegrated. He lives alone in a small, cheap apartment near the campus where he cooks rice and vegetables in a single saucepan, drinks vodka and reads books on esoteric subjects."[12] Tormented by tooth problems, Don Jr. begins to have adventures in his imagination. He decides that he was really called to the college as a pretext for some other mission, and he searches personal ads for clues. He finds one that says only, "Higher than eagles he wanted to learn to fly," and he calls the number. He is given instructions to proceed to the Mexican border, at which point he finds himself taken under the wing of a series of Don Juan–like guides. An Indian takes him on a wild ride through the desert, leaving him twelve times to be picked up by "the man," who keeps failing to show up. Losing the ability to tell past from present, Don Jr. begins reliving earlier parts of his life. Finally the man meets him in a crowded place and, instead of teaching him about premonitions as expected, gives his political lectures on the economics of oppression. The man, "not ironical like Castaneda's Don Juan," as the text mentions, is an uncivilized screamer who wants to go back to the practice of communal ownership of land.

All this is actually taking place in Don Jr.'s apartment, of course. Ashley's synopsis ends, "We will never find out what happens to Don Jr. . . . Maybe he will go into writing screenplays,"[13] which is what Ashley attempted toward the end of his Mills College experience.

Foreign Experiences is in four eighteen-minute acts:

1. The Flying Serpent
2. The Jaguar
3. The Coyote
4. Eagle Tearing Hearts Out of Chests

"The Flying Serpent" opens with Don Jr. and his family and N arriving at the college, metaphorized as El Dorado, and going in at what's now called the back gate because they don't use it anymore. They realize that the place is haunted. Don Jr. enunciates a theory that "the skin is the (so-called) soul" and that "a break in the skin lets in spirits" (15). Ashley refers to reading Immanuel Velikovsky (1895–1979), a highly controversial writer who tried to reconcile chronologies of ancient Egypt, Greece, and Israel, and in the process argued that catastrophic events (such as the entry of Venus into the solar system) had happened within recorded history. Shunned and ostracized by the scientific community in the 1970s (and since) for his books *Worlds in Collision* (1950) and *Earth in Upheaval* (1955), Velikovsky was subsequently declared correct in some of his predictions, such as his claim (hotly debated at the time) that the dinosaurs disappeared suddenly because of a cataclysm. The line that expresses Ashley's admiration for him is, "He writes ideas fuck your approval that has its charms" (19).

Don Jr., "secret scientist of the occult" [act 3, lines 17–18], demonstrates the results of his research to some senators. (We're not told the subject of this research, but we should assume, because of Don Jr.'s main obsession, that the secret research concerns premonitions.) This perhaps reflects the foundation money that Ashley got to build up the electronic studio at Mills. Don Jr. and family start off on a Southwest vacation—"Don considers his options while Linda's in the bathroom" (22) is by now a resonant line—and considers, in lines quoted at the start of chapter 1, the problem of researching why the British don't have oral sex. In a dream, apparently, Don Jr. sees himself as Giordano Bruno being burned at the stake, asked to recant by "Some asshole in a fancy suit."

Near the beginning of act 2, "The Jaguar," is a dialogue between Don Jr. and Linda reminiscent of their encounters at the airline ticket counter in *Improvement*, with questions and answers stated simultaneously, as in a ritual. Don Jr. wants to go to the Mexican border to meet the guide, and Linda, with a woman's subtle logic of desperation, tries hard to dissuade him:

> She speaks to me and I to her:
> Don't you think this is unfair to me?
> I guess so.
> In other words, this is all you?
> More important than us together.
> Not more important.
> More important, if I have no say in it.
> What you've said has changed it.
> What I've said hasn't made you more cautious.
> It has made me more cautious.
> This is not what I would call caution . . .
> The consequences are not trivial for me.
> Nor for me. That's what I'm afraid of . . .
> I have to go now. I love you.
> Fuck that kind of love. I love you, too.
> Don't drink the water.
> Good-bye. (36–38)

Lines 221 to 248 (with a couple of one-verse reprises following) offer the opera's pop song, in which the first, third, and fourth lines are the same in every verse. The entire song takes place over a G-flat major 7th chord, with the capitalized line chanted on a high F:

> Baby's off the magic powders
> She don't like a good mood all that much
> Nothing getting done for me
> VERY GREAT HIP BOOK I KEEP IT BY MY BED
>
> Baby's off the magic powders
> She just couldn't get unloaded
> Nothing getting done for me
> VERY GREAT HIP BOOK I KEEP IT BY MY BED (39)

As this blares on the radio, Don Jr. and the Indian are driving along in a pickup truck ("the ordinariness is more than I expected"). The Indian speculates about the possibility of not turning the wheel and crashing into the rock, a Clint Eastwood–type sheriff appearing in the aftermath to deconstruct the accident.

In act 3, "The Coyote," Don Jr. finds himself having to learn to curse. The lines "This discovery that, / As the man said, is the tune, / Not the words, came as a strange relief" (54) seem to be a reference to the Mark Twain anecdote in which his wife tried to shame him by repeating his swear words to him, and he replied, "You have the words, my dear, but I'm afraid you'll never master the tune." What Don Jr. wants, though, is to learn about premonitions, his research project:

> We live in a constant state of premonition, of course.
> Personally, I always knew this. Everybody does.
> Officially, it's treated like a well-kept secret.
> Nobody cares why, and for good reason.
> It's too deep, so facetious serves[.] (55–56)

Ashley makes an argument for the mathematical form of premonitions: that just as the two sides of an equation have to be equal, the content of a premonition must equal that of the event that follows it. The problem, he continues, is that

> The confirmation of the
> Fact that the equation works always mostly
> Comes in another language, and languages don't
> Always match. For instance, since the proof is
> Mathematical, which is not spoken, the
> Confirmation, say it's anecdotal, which is
> Always spoken, takes too long, so we
> Don't believe it[.] (57)

He describes, in the circuitous manner of Ashley's conversational style, a couple of autobiographical premonitions he had in his own life. At line 165 the text suddenly breaks into the text of *Purposeful Lady Slow Afternoon*. A hallucination of Eleanor contains the line "She was a visitor" (68), and his fantasy of meeting her in a restaurant turns into a description of the plot from *eL/Aficionado*. He finally meets "the Promised Man," who is "permanently pissed off" and "not civilized" (71).

Act 4 begins with the promised man's lecture on economics. The principle is that people who start an industry entice other investors, giving "the feeling that / The whole industry is working together toward a goal" (78) and then at some point the most powerful people take over and cut the less powerful out of the money. The man thinks the phrase "If you have to ask you can't afford one" should be carved along the bottom of "that stupid / Mountain with the four guys['] heads" (80), a reference to Mount Rushmore. Words, as the epistemology continues, "don't have no meaning they are just a uniform / You put on to get you in a certain line of work" (85). The lecture closes—though without conclusion—with some of the same ideas about agriculture and architecture broached in *Perfect Lives*—in fact, with a ninety-nine-line text that was originally intended for *Perfect Lives* but that was omitted and became a separate entity titled "Ideas from the Church." Indeed, we never find out what happens to Don Jr.

Foreign Experiences uses the same jazz chords (or rather, fourteen of the sixteen) used in *eL/Aficionado*; these are more audible in the quieter second and third acts and are somewhat drowned out in the first by the Piano Sonata in the background and in the fourth by the running bass line. Reciting tones for the voices are drawn from these chords, although in performance there is much freedom of inflection. Pacing of the chord changes is irregular, though in the first three acts the most common duration is eighteen measures. In act 4 the pacing is generally faster, and there are two passages (lines 84–153 and 224–30) where the music cycles quickly through a seven-chord sequence, one chord per line. The text is marked off into scenes, and in act 1 the ending of these scenes is noted by the narrator. The scenes are not outlined by the harmony, and analysis suggests that the temporal aspects of music and text were arrived at independently.

Yellow Man with Heart with Wings, the 1990 recording that underlies act 4, is itself based on the text "Ideas from the Church." This separate recording resulted from a commission from radio station KUNM-FM in Albuquerque. The piece is an audio realization of *in memoriam . . . KIT CARSON (Opera)*; Ashley was going to apply that title to it, but American Indians in Albuquerque objected to the reference. The *Kit Carson* score calls for eighty-one events with given stop and start times, which Ashley applied to the synthesizer tones that underlie the text. For the Lovely Music recording, he assembled two versions, the first with the text read in Spanish by Guillermo Grenier, the second with the English text read by Ashley, but so heavily processed as to be barely comprehensible. The whole is underlaid with a soft, ambient, consonant electronic background by Tyranny playing a Clavinet.

Now Eleanor's Idea

The final opera in the tetralogy *Now Eleanor's Idea* documents Ashley's involvement with the lowrider community around Española and Chimayó in northern New Mexico. A lowrider is a car (often a classic 1950s car, Chevy Impalas, Monte Carlos, and Cadillacs being popular)[14] that has had its suspension system altered to ride lower than normal. Often the car is decorated with an extremely detailed pictorial paint job, often with religious significance. (The term *lowrider* also refers to the men who work on and drive such cars.) Cultural artifacts such as *Lowrider* magazine (founded 1977)[15] tend to involve continual juxtaposition of such cars with beautiful young women in bikinis. Ashley went to Chimayó, site of one of the oldest Spanish missions in the United States and reputed to be the site of the spiritual origins of the lowrider culture, in 1993, and obtained an introduction to a lowrider named Dennis Martinez. Through Martinez he was able to spend considerable time among the lowriders, whose cars he sees as an authentic and important subcategory of Catholic iconography. When *Now Eleanor's Idea* was performed at the Greer Garson Theater in Santa Fe from August 3 to August 6, 1995, Martinez and Julian Quintana organized a concurrent lowrider car show in the theater parking lot.

Compared to its predecessors, *Now Eleanor's Idea* is a relatively linear story whose plot is right on the surface, though delivered in two languages, English and Spanish. Somewhat like the prologue to Wagner's *Götterdämmerung* (and here's the only *Ring of the Nibelungs* comparison in this book), act 1 of *Now Eleanor's Idea*, "Change," starts by recapping the past. The story of the temporary bank robbery from *Perfect Lives* is here narrated by Ashley in a much more linear fashion than it was there, and from Now Eleanor's point of view. Now Eleanor has the "approach of the end of the world feeling," which strikes men every fourteen years and women every ten years. (Ashley read this idea in the 1970s in a book on India. He can no longer find the reference, but he does believe that the lows and highs in his life run in a fourteen-year cycle.) The fight of the dogs, the woman throwing water on the bank manager, and the realization that the money is no longer in the vault are described, and Now Eleanor is in love with the man (Buddy) she suspects is Mexican. The flash of light she experiences at that moment makes her realize she must quit her job. "The decision takes less time / Than the word immediately can describe" (lines 281–82).

Serendipitously, an old flame who now works at a television station calls and offers Now Eleanor a job as an anchorwoman on the nightly news.

> He remembered
> Now Eleanor as unusually comely,
> And yet reassuring in her
> Appearance, not exotic at all, and
> Well-read and knowing how to pronounce
> Most words. . . .
> . . . She has the not rare but highly
> Prized gift of to think in speech. She does not
> Separate the two. In Now Eleanor
> Mind and body are united. [lines 350–55, 378–81][16]

Now Eleanor is an instant celebrity. She decides, though, to research and solve the bank robbery and to head for a month to El Dorado, the land of miracles, to find the Mexican. In the last twenty-four lines of Act I, Now Eleanor introduces herself to her listeners and declares the reappearance of the money in the bank itself a kind of miracle.

In musical terms, act 1 is low-key and unusually minimalist. It cycles through eight chords, mostly sus chords (chords with an unresolving perfect fourth above the bass), in unvarying sequence in a four-flat key signature; the prominence of A-flat as a reciting tone sometimes suggests a D-flat major tonality. Six of the eight chords have no accidentals but vary the bass note (B♭, C, E♭, G, F, A♭), creating an overall effect harmonically similar to that of Steve Reich's *Music for 18 Musicians* (1976), in which subtle harmonic variety within a constant diatonic scale is also created via changing bass tones. These eight chords are also the ones that characterize the opera as a whole. Chords 2 through 4 will mark off the three scenes of act 2, chords 5 through 7 will differentiate the three scenes of act 3, and chord 8 will suffice for the entire final act.

Act 2, "The Miracle of Cars," is in three clearly demarcated scenes. The first (0:00–3:00) and the third (21:00–22:00) are monologues by Now Eleanor; the much longer middle scene uses interviews Ashley did with his lowrider friends in New Mexico. Chanting on B♭, then G, then C, then E♭ over a C minor 7 chord, Now Eleanor introduces herself for her television audience and tells them she has fallen in love with their cars. When she announces, "I call this program 'The Miracle of Cars,'" scene 2 opens with a burst of energy, a widening of the sonic space, and an increase in the number of layers. Over an E-flat sus chord the chorus sings in Spanish, as though over car radios in car shops, a discourse on the Seven Ages of the Three Great Families, Jews, Hispanics, and Whites, "divorced in time and divorced in space" (48) and who are meeting in the great future in Los Angeles. The ages we have lived through are as follows:

First: The Age of Single Language, experience embodied in icons
Second: The Age of Purposeful Movement, learned advantages of reciprocity in pairing
Third: The Age of Caring, principle of attachment, architecture
Fourth: The Age of Waiting, agriculture, name separate from the presence of the thing
Fifth: The Age of On the Other Hand, argument, differentiation, separation
Sixth: The Age of Reproduction, technology, learning by mistake

We are now in the Sixth Age: in the Seventh, "the east-west paths will disappear." The Three Great Families are surrounded, shackled, engulfed by contingencies. They are divorced from enduring things, because

We must be home to have enduring things,
Which are pacifiers of the mind.

> Enduring things make a home for you . . .
> Our acceptance of homelessness is so much a part of life here now
> That we recognize homelessness as the root of heroism. (48–49)

This learned and all-explaining discourse is in Spanish and mostly backgrounded (sung in the background beneath other text), but it will reappear in English as "The Song" in act 4. Placed over it, starting at 4:30, is a taped interview with a lowrider named Arthur "LowLow" Medina and his girlfriend Joan. LowLow narrates a story of having decorated his own lowrider car, becoming discouraged with it, spray-painting it black, selling it, and then falling into deep depression. Then a friend located the original car, and LowLow obtained it and spent seven years restoring it to its original decorated condition. Meanwhile, in another sound layer, every six measures Joan La Barbara sings a thrillingly slow glissando from one of the pitches A♭, B♭, D♭, and E♭ to one of the others, and that glissando is echoed and overlapped by another singer, Amy X Neuberg (a West Coast composer and performance artist). The act's one-minute dénouement returns to the C minor-7 chord, over which La Barbara thanks her viewers for teaching her about the beauty of their cars, in a pitch sequence F–G–C–B♭–E♭ that changes pitch at the appearance of each Spanish phrase.

Act 3, "Questions and Answers," was inspired by *Lowrider* magazine's advice to the lovelorn column, written in a fluid mix of Spanish and English by one Tia Chucha. "The Miracle of Cars" has been so successful that people start calling in to ask Now Eleanor questions—some of them about cars, but more and more about life problems. Ashley narrates this in a three-minute introduction, and then sample questions are asked by various voices, and La Barbara answers them. The first question slyly alludes to *eL/Aficionado*: it's from someone whose brother asked him to sit in a restaurant and describe into the phone people going into a building. Others are on more general issues of race and marriage. More and more the questions and answers morph from English into Spanish, until the last is almost entirely in Spanish. In a postlude, Ashley breaks in to explain that after a while Now Eleanor can't go on.

> There are too many silences.
> Everybody is listening,
> And there are great silences on the air.
> No music. No weather. No advertising.
> Just great silences,
> With all the listeners and watchers
> Thinking together, as if in prayer . . .
> It became more and more apparent that

> Now Eleanor was the "face" of the people,
> Almost a kind of mask through which
> The voice could speak without hesitation or fear. (105)

Finally, Now Eleanor announces her last show and explains that she's been asked to sing a song kept alive from the distant past, one that someone is asked to sing in every generation to release the people from unhappiness.

Act 4 is "The Song," the text of which we have already heard in act 2, though now it is in English and in the foreground. It is identified as "the song of the meeting of the Three Great Families of the Most High Desert Reaches," which in turn are specified as the Climbing Roses Have Covered the Wall on the Dark Side of the House family, the Snake Sleeps in the Sun family, and the Metal Roof Holds the Memory of Thunder Lightly family. In this Ashley has set himself a task something like the challenge Wagner posed himself in *Tannheuser* and *Die Meistersinger*: within the context of opera, a song is set off and promised as special, so it must raise the music to a new level. Ashley answers this challenge by unleashing La Barbara from the usual chanting tones to freely improvise around an A-flat Mixolydian mode (A♭ B♭ C D♭ E♭ F G♭), making this the most extended melodic passage in any of the operas. Choral interruptions and increased activity among the rattling drones in the orchestra engender increased excitement. The final judgment delivered on the song by the chorus is hardly comforting:

> This summarizes all that we can know.
> There is no before and after "outside."
> There is no before the Seven Ages.
> There is no after the Seven Ages . . .
> The sixth age is no wiser than the first.
> To interpret this accounting as such
> Would be the gravest misunderstanding.
> We are in the sixth age and remember.
> Remembering is accumulation. It
> is not wisdom, unfortunately. . . .
> What is "passed down" to us is memory.
> Its value has yet to be determined.
> It is passed down to us as obstruction.
> A darkening of the sky at midday.
> A multiplicity of ways to choose.
> A lore of wisdom that is untested.
> An accumulation of misjudgments. (128–29)

Now Eleanor's Idea was premiered, along with the tetralogy as a whole, in Avignon, France, at the Festival d'Avignon at the Théâtre Municipal, July 19–23, 1994. Other complete performances have been presented at the Palais des Fêtes in Strasbourg (October 4–5, 1994), at the Brooklyn Academy of Music (November 16–19, 1994), and at the Greer Garson Theater in Santa Fe (August 3–6, 1995).

I should mention the quasi-symphonic overall shape of the entire tetralogy. Mirroring the four movements of a symphony, *Improvement* is the most complex, variable, and detailed; *eL/Aficionado* is a kind of low-density "slow movement"; *Foreign Experiences* is more manic and at a faster tempo, like a scherzo; and *Now Eleanor's Idea* is an impressive finale, with layer upon layer of activity. These correspondences extend not only to musical qualities but also to the subject matter. The Russian music theorist Mark Aranovsky has characterized the four movements of a typical symphony as representing *Homo agens* (man acting, or in conflict), *Homo sapiens* (man thinking), *Homo ludens* (man playing), and *Homo communis* (man in the community).[17] These four categories correlate to the four parts of *Now Eleanor's Idea* remarkably well, and in the traditional order:

1. *Homo agens*	*Improvement*, Linda in conflict and acting to ensure her own safety
2. *Homo sapiens*	*eL/Aficionado*, the agent looking back and trying to reconcile his experiences
3. *Homo ludens*	*Foreign Experiences*, Don Jr. having wild rides with an Indian guide in his imagination
4. *Homo communis*	*Now Eleanor's Idea*, Now Eleanor finding her destiny within the lowrider community

Responding subconsciously to ancient archetypes, Ashley has given us a great operatic symphony.

8

One Thing Follows the Next and I Just Do It

Dust, *Celestial Excursions*, *Concrete*, and Smaller Pieces

WHEN I INTERVIEWED ASHLEY IN 1991 prior to the New York premieres of *Improvement* and *eL/Aficionado*, he astounded me by telling me he had already created the narrative framework for his next fifty operas. What that meant, it turned out, was that he had come up with forty-nine titles for what he was calling "The Immortality Songs," spin-off operas that would constitute radio shows done by Junior Jr. Ashley has a serious obsession with the number seven, and the requirement for each title was that it be seven syllables. Since 1991 Ashley has written works for about one-half of these titles, including *Yellow Man with Heart with Wings*, *When Famous Last Words Fail You*, and *Your Money My Life Goodbye*. Others he is still looking forward to using, such as "A Bullet-Proof Nun Arrives," "Vegetarians on Trial," and "Mixed Blessings, Indiana."[1]

In the late 1980s and 1990s, increased involvement with performers and an increased profile in the New York and European performance scenes brought Ashley a series of nonoperatic commissions, including three rather sizable nonvocal works. For the flutist Barbara Held (at that time living with Buckner) Ashley wrote a flute concerto called *Superior Seven* (1988); for the Relache ensemble in Philadelphia, tireless promoters of nontraditional chamber music, he wrote *Outcome Inevitable* (1991); and for the pianist Lois Svard, on the faculty of Bucknell University in Pennsylvania, he wrote the piano piece *Van Cao's Meditation* (1992).

At Buckner's suggestion he also wrote, or one might say completed, in 1992, a wordless vocal piece with orchestra called *Tract*, based on an unrealized idea from 1955. And at Buckner's urging, the American Composers Orchestra commissioned from Ashley a work for voices and orchestra called *When Famous Last Words Fail You* (1997). Later he received two commissions from Holland's expert Ensemble MAE, *Tap Dancing in the Sand* (2004) and *Hidden Similarities* (2005).

For practical purposes, Ashley writes, *Superior Seven* is unplayable for the orchestra in its current state, and the recording released on New World Records is a MIDI version with electronic instruments, over which Held plays live flute. The core of the piece is a piano line in a succession of single notes from which the rest of the orchestra takes its cues and with which some instruments play certain notes in unison. The cue notes are chosen in a kind of elaborate *soggetto cavato*, a correspondence between notes and letters, following a series of home advertisements Ashley picked from the *New York Times*. Some of these are already familiar from their interpolation into the text of *eL/Aficionado*:

From the moment you step inside this elegant
    (spacious) prewar home
You will instantly appreciate
    its flowing (and gracious)
Floor plan oversized
    (high ceilinged) rooms
Three bedrooms
    (three baths).[2]

The piano line bases its notes on this succession of letters according to an eccentric scheme that assigns certain notes the same letter. For instance, the first F is a high B, the R an F, O an A, M a lower F, T an A within the treble clef, and so on. The key between letters and pitches changes as the harmony changes. From the listener's point of view, the sequence is fairly random.

Superior Seven can be played by ensembles of different sizes, the smallest consisting of just piano, flute, viola, and electronic organ. Potentially there are seven ensembles playing at once. Instruments take their cues from the piano part, whose tempo is not fixed, and the conductor does not beat time but merely adjusts volumes among the groups, while the flutist plays arabesques based on the available pitches. The result, on the New World recording at least, is a dark, tonal, atmospheric continuum on a rhythmic grid. Its closest relatives in the repertoire might be Cage's early orchestra piece *The Seasons* and certain works of Lou Harrison, which share its meandering progress through a pleasantly enigmatic tonality.

Along with *Superior Seven*, Ashley revised and electronically realized a work he had started and abandoned in 1955 called *Tract*. Ashley's idea at the time was to create a five-line polyphony in which the implied harmony was not always present but was obscured by unresolved suspensions. He thought of the result as a "harmonic aura," whose actual harmonic content would change depending on what timbres were used. In 1992 Buckner encouraged him to complete the work for voice and electronics in place of orchestra. Ashley originally had a text in mind—excerpts from poems by Wallace Stevens—but his thinking had evolved so far from that kind of text-setting that he completed the piece with wordless vocals. He also found that he needed to include the implied harmonies as a background to make the piece make sense. In any case, *Tract* is a moody, atmospheric, darkly attractive piece of abstract music.

Outcome Inevitable is a relatively simple piece for Ashley, and one of his most engaging instrumental works. It is scored almost conventionally, though, for Relache's unusual ensemble of flute, oboe, saxophone, bassoon, electronic keyboard, percussion, viola, and bass. (Ashley invites reorchestrations for other instruments, and the Ensemble MAE has recorded the work in a different version.) The piece is grounded in an insistent repeating middle C in the bass, in constant sixteenth notes. The structure is set by repeating rhythms tapped out softly on a bass drum in odd groupings: first a 7+10 pattern (counted in sixteenth notes), then 3+3+3+3+5+3+5, and so on. Because the number of sixteenth notes in each pattern is odd, the repetitions have to occur in multiples of four so that the section will end at the end of a measure. These rhythms create a seven-part structure, each part of which accompanies a solo by a different instrument; see table 3. It will be apparent that the oboist doubles on English horn, the clarinetist on soprano sax, and the flutist on alto flute.

TABLE 3. Rhythms in *Outcome Inevitable*

Soloist	Drum Pattern	Pattern length	No. of repetitions	Section length
Oboe	7+10	= 17 𝅘𝅥𝅯	× 28	119 ♩
Flute	3+3+3+3+5+3+5	= 25	× 24	150
Clarinet	3+3+4+5+8	= 23	× 28	161
Alto flute	3+10+2+8	= 23	× 28	161
English horn	4+4+5+2+2+4	= 21	× 32	168
Soprano sax	9+4+2+3+7	= 25	× 24	150
Bassoon	17+5+3	= 25	× 32	200

The melodic aspect of these solos is quite simple in concept and beautiful to follow. Almost all of the melodies consist merely of rising scales interrupted by occasional leaps (or steps) downward to keep the line within a fairly narrow range. Each phrase consists of a number of sixteenth notes (from 0 to 6) leading to a sustained note. The sustained notes have durations divisible by a dotted quarter note, from 1 to 7. The sustained notes are also accompanied by chords in the electric keyboard (basically drawn from the chords for *eL/Aficionado* and *Foreign Experiences*, though revoiced), and "shadowed" by a note in the viola that starts in unison in the first section and moves a step further away in each section. Lasting sixteen minutes, the piece is a lovely evocation of timelessness, drawn from a clear and endlessly elaborated idea but quite unpredictable in its details. Relache premiered the piece May 12 1991, at New York's Bang on a Can festival.

Van Cao's Meditation is based just as constantly—one might say as minimalistically—on the same permutational scheme. The piece was inspired by a photo Ashley saw in *National Geographic* of an old Vietnamese man named Van Cao, composer of the country's national anthem, sitting at what was apparently one of only two pianos in the country at the time. Ashley listened to some of Van Cao's music (songs in a French cabaret style) and imagined what he wanted to hear Van Cao playing. The piece consists of a steady stream of single notes using only the pitches B♭, C, D♭, E♭, and F♭, with an occasional *ppp* cadence on an A♭ in octaves. The pianist is supposed to continually alternate hands, making the work choreographic and quite difficult, since many lines leap around the keyboard in octaves. Svard premiered the work at the St. Louis Art Museum on April 18, 1993.

For decades after leaving graduate school, Ashley never wrote for orchestra—*Superior Seven* and *Tract* were attempts to write for an electronic orchestra of his own imagination—but in 1997 Buckner secured him a commission from the American Composers Orchestra in New York. The result, *When Famous Last Words Fail You*, became the source of a bitter disappointment. The piece was a text for Buckner as soloist with La Barbara, Humbert, and Sam Ashley as an interjecting chorus. It is a whimsical story about the invention of a "youth salve" that ensured immortality, but with the unwanted side effect that people who used it completely lost their identities and became someone else entirely:

> those were the days. I myself saw the
> person I understood to be my own grandmother playing
> second base for the New York Team for three seasons before,
> incredibly, during the brief period of a pinch-running chore,
> over twenty million viewers, it is said, saw the organism

> change into what appeared to be, before the umpires got the game stopped, a decrepit sharecropper.[3]

The performance problem was that the orchestral instruments were all supposed to play only the pitch A, in different octaves and in different timbres (flutter-tongue, and so on), and to be cued by words in the text. The conductor's job was not to beat time but merely to adjust volume levels. Dennis Russell Davies, the conductor, apparently didn't like this. After sight-reading through the piece once, he canceled further rehearsals and, in Carnegie Hall on December 7, 1997, gave what Ashley considered a miserable and misleading performance. There has not yet been another with orchestra, though Ashley has had the text performed in more modest circumstances.

In 2004 the Ensemble MAE in Holland (so named because it had been the Maarten Altena Ensemble until the director retired) commissioned a piece from Ashley, for which he returned to a text he had written in 1979. At that time the experimental video artist Woody Vasulka had asked Ashley to play the role of the nineteenth-century composer Hector Berlioz in a video opera; Ashley was to be seen speaking, but his words would not be heard, so he merely needed a profound-looking piece of oratory. Since he was reading Frances Yates's work about the theater of memory, he chose some texts from the book used to develop memory. But the text for *Tap Dancing in the Sand*, as the Ensemble MAE piece came to be titled, is a musing by someone sitting at breakfast at a Holiday Inn and thinking about Cicero and other great orators:

> According to Cicero,
> Whoever he is,
> Only people with
> A powerful memory
> Know what they intend
> To say
> And for how
> Long they are going to speak,
> And in what style, and
> What points
> They have already answered,
> And what still remains.[4]

As in *Superior Seven* he created a code that would match the syllables to pitches, specifically from middle C down to the F♯ below, and distributed lines among the instruments. Ashley usually performs the voice part himself when Ensemble

MAE does the piece. It's a calm, cute work with an arrhythmic accompaniment in parallel major triads.

Your Money My Life Goodbye (1998)

One of the immortality songs, *Your Money My Life Goodbye* is a kind of satire about white-collar crime, even more timely today than when it was written. As usual, the piece is drawn from life. The inspiration started with a letter that was forwarded to Mimi by her mother about one of her mother's classmates saying she couldn't come to her class reunion, but she was sending her son, who, from the elaborate description, was obviously a spy. Ashley loved the letter and used its beginning to start off the opera. At the same time, he had read stories in the *New York Times* about Michele Sindona, a crooked financier who in 1985 was sentenced to twelve years in prison for having stolen $130 million from the Vatican. A news report about a Russian spy who stole NATO secrets by romancing a NATO secretary completed the picture, and Ashley wove the whole into a startling but not improbable story.

The libretto takes the form of a letter written by an unnamed woman in response to an invitation to her school's class reunion. She can't go because she's recovering from some unspecified medical problem, but she's sending her son C-III, who we understand from her description to be an international spy. In the course of the letter we learn that C-III's wife, Ms. Ona, has just died of cyanide poisoning in a Chicago hospital. She was an internationally known financier and swindler whose dealings caused the failing of banks in the United States and Europe and who was convicted of contracting the murder of a former employee who was about to expose her. Whether Ms. Ona was murdered or committed suicide is unclear. (In 1986 Sindona likewise died of cyanide poisoning, whether by murder or suicide.)[5] As Ashley concludes in the program notes, "*Your Money My Life Goodbye* doesn't take this seriously at all. Everybody is crazy."[6]

Jacqueline Humbert, as the woman who wrote the letter, reads the parts of the letter in which she speaks for herself. Joan La Barbara speaks the lines that are quotations from Ms. Ona. Ashley reads the newspaper accounts included with the letter for documentation, and other lines are given to Sam Ashley and Tom Buckner. The score is one of Ashley's most minimalist works, based throughout on a series of pulsing chords in A-flat major (four flats again) at ♪ = 216. Quite remarkably, the text is divided into 892 lines of seven syllables each (divided 3 + 2 + 2 in the score, reflecting the rhythm of the title line) and so carefully constructed that no words are ever hyphenated from one line to the next; in other words, it is a poem entirely (or almost, as there are a few rests) composed of groups of words totaling seven syllables:

A wild am-	bition	to be
someone else,	to have	a masked,
secret life	that en-	livens
a drab and	grey ex-	istence,
is often	more im-	portant.[7]

Every line is supposed to be intoned in the same inflection and accent pattern as the title, *Your Money My Life Goodbye*. Yet there are fifteen pulsing chords in the orchestra per vocal line. Increasingly toward the end a bass ostinato groups the chords into 6/4 patterns in a syncopated eighth-note pattern of 6 + 3 + 3 + 3 + 6 + 3. The relationship of vocal lines to musical phrases, then (new text line every fifteen pulsations, new rhythmic ostinato every twenty-four pulsations), is fairly complex, and it forestalls any clear perception of the repeating seven-syllable scheme.

Dust (1998)

Dust, *Celestial Excursions*, and *Concrete* form a trilogy of mostly autobiographical operas dealing with groups of people marginalized from society and unrelated to the *Perfect Lives* storyline. *Dust* is one of Ashley's most personal, least abstract, most endearing operas. Absent is the kind of overarching historical reference or underlying theoretical construct we find in the earlier trilogy. Written when Ashley was sixty-eight, *Dust* takes old age as part of its subject matter, as will the other two. The narrator (Ashley) plays the character of one of six homeless people who live in a park—in Tribeca Park, in fact, across the street from Ashley's apartment.[8]

The park is a triangle.
It's maybe 120 feet on the long side.
Hundred feet on one side. Sixty feet on the other.
Maybe it's bigger. I can't do the arithmetic.
There are ten benches. (11)

Ashley says that this was a true description of the park when he was writing *Dust*, but with Mayor David Bloomberg's improvement programs there are now more than twenty benches (and fewer visible homeless). Most significant, *Dust* brings to a climax Ashley's narrative fascination with characters considered outcasts, a concern that goes back to the 1959 film *The Bottleman*.

In terms of harmonic language and narrative style, *Dust* represents a deliberate simplification relative to the *Now Eleanor's Idea* operas; the chords are triadic, the stories linear and easily followed. In one respect, though, Ashley took on a new level of complexity: the layering of different texts at the same time. The story sections have a background text and a foreground text at the same time, and in the "No Legs" scene, the story of a man who lost his legs in some war, Ashley tries out a quick "hocketing" technique of lines quickly overlapping from one voice to another. As he admits, "Any listener (the audience) is offended by and resents being forced to give attention to more than one source of spoken (or sung) information, if there is no 'hierarchy' to this information. Two sentences at the same time is bad. This is a fact. It is a deep, biological adaptation, which protects us from harm."[9] But Ashley still wanted to have many stories in play at once, and his answer here, in "No Legs," is to have a principal singer (himself) on the beat, "chased" by four others whose voices are triggered by the first and rotate in rapid sequence.

There are six characters in *Dust*, one of whom is never heard from—all of them based on homeless people Ashley saw living in Tribeca Park. The main narrator is nameless, listed merely as "I live in the park." An unheard character called No Legs is a veteran of an unnamed war who lost his legs, lives in a wheelchair, and likes to sing. It is his stories that the other five characters sing ("So we are going to sing a few of his songs, perfectly"). The Man in the Green Pants (Sam Ashley) yells at cops as they go by, "I am the president of mother-fuckers against drunk driving!" Lucille (Joan La Barbara, playing a homeless woman who had appeared in *Perfect Lives*) used to be pretty, but now she yells six hours a day, and a man in the diner gives her sandwiches. The Rug (Tom Buckner) sleeps on a bench wrapped in a big waterproof rug he found. ("He is the envy of everybody. Rain doesn't bother him at all.") And Shirley Temple (Jacqueline Humbert) is so called because when she was a child she was a stand-in for the famous child actress.

Ashley begins with some musings about art, occasioned by his trips to what sounds like the Metropolitan Museum:

> First thing
> You notice is how much work it took to make these things.
> Lots of people. Lots of time. Very impressive.
> Like cathedrals and that kind of thing.
> Next thing you notice is how nobody in the museum cares.
> I'm the only person who is actually looking . . .
> Everybody else is just walking around.
> Thirty seconds here, thirty seconds there. How nice.

I get the idea. The whole thing is traffic.
It's like a huge dance
Made up by the guy who decided where to put things . . .
Finally, well, honey, it's been a couple of hours. I think
We got our money's worth. You know where the bus stop is?
Actually, getting there and getting home
Is more interesting than what's in the museum.
That's why they go. Got to keep moving. (9–10)

Ashley describes his friends in terms of their "irreversabilities" (*sic*), that is, things that are wrong with them that they can't change:

But the friend who lost a couple of legs in some war has
Definite irreversabilities. We don't grow back legs.
So he's kind of a hero in the park.
His irreversabilities are real.
He doesn't have to feel like it could be changed
With a little exercise of the will.
He doesn't have to think of himself as a fuck-up. (19)

The accompaniment to this fifteen-minute introduction consists of a non-repeating series of conventional chords that will recur through the rest of the opera. Though the conventional chord progression (A♭–B♭7–C7–f–A♭–E♭–B–E–c♯–d♯–A–E–f♯, and so on) doesn't repeat, its rhythm does, in a seventeen-measure isorhythm of 1, 2, 3, 5, 3, 2, and 1 measures, expanding and contracting via the first few numbers of the Fibonacci series. At the end of the introduction, Ashley announces that the group is going to sing four of the songs by the man in the wheelchair. All are stories from Ashley's youth. Each story is 224 four-beat lines long and lasts nine minutes and fifty-seven seconds. They are sung by the four soloists as follows:

Theosophy	Jacqueline Humbert
The Priest	Sam Ashley
If There's Anything . . .	Joan La Barbara
The Little Gun	Thomas Buckner

The tempo now is ♩ = 90 bpm, four beats per line. The chord changes happen at different rates in each song:

Theosophy	every	16	lines/measures
The Priest	"	8	"
If There's Anything . . .	"	18	"
The Little Gun	"	37	"

Elsewhere Ashley explains that the songs are all the same length because they are based on a chant that runs underneath all four solos.[10] The chant, a background of chords whose words are barely distinguishable, describes No Legs's wartime experiences, especially the recovery from losing his legs. This is as close to stream-of-consciousness as Ashley's prose gets, though (while the war is not named) it resembles something like the chaotic dialogue in a battle scene of a Vietnam War film. There are references to morphine and to the "pizza delivery guy," or medic, who comes around with the "peanuts" whose end is bitten off to expose the needle to be plunged into the flesh of the suffering victim. Bitter humor and despair alternate: "No more dancing, man. / Just watching, you know." "I'm losing it. F'hing channel is fading out." "Where's the peanut guy?"

"Theosophy" tells of riding around with the tough theosophy guy who wanted to marry Ashley's sister, and "The Little Gun" is about buying a gun to scare off two men near the army base who were intimidating Mary; both stories are recounted in chapter 2. "The Priest" tells of five priests Ashley used to socialize with at their church in Oakland in the 1970s. One evening the one Ashley knows the best takes him to a Mexican restaurant where he seemed to be the most popular and important person there. Afterward, the priest takes Ashley out to the docks at night, and it dawns on Ashley that the priest may subtly be looking for sexual involvement:

> I am beginning to get an idea.
> I probably have my hands in my pockets.
> My friend is lonely.
> He is probably lonelier than I am.
> This is an important moment for me.
> I don't get ideas like this very often.
> I am starting to get confused.
> I mean, about what is supposed to happen next.
> I feel like I have to do something.
> But I don't know what it is.
> Normally I don't get confused.
> Probably because I am so dumb.
> One thing follows the next and I just do it.
> I never think about the consequences.
> Now the consequences are right in front of me.
> All I can think about is the consequences.
> Now, I am trying to figure out who I am.
> Which is not easy for a person of my intelligence. (50–51)

"If there's anything . . ." is a rather embarrassing, and therefore shockingly honest, story about Ashley as a teenager with two friends stumbling across two gay men making love in the park, who summarily beat the heck out of them. (The title comes from what one of the gay men says before the fight: "If there's anything I like better than sucking cock, it's fighting.") The episode occasions a digression about a time Ashley was dropping acid on a beach with friends, wandered away, and saw a heterosexual couple making love. Ashley personifies the self-consciousness such images bring as "the outside guy":

> It divided me. It made me into two people.
> The guy doing it and the guy watching.
> It's been one of my problems with life.
> Like I can't stand to see people eat. (64)

Following "The Little Gun" Ashley gives a brief prologue to "No Legs," explaining that they're now going to sing No Legs's songs. Then in a texture unlike any in Ashley's previous music, Ashley sings No Legs's song as the other singers respond quickly in mini-cascades of poetry:

> R.A.: Now he got the peanuts
> T.B.: the pizza delivery boy
> J.H.: our favorite man
> S.A.: don't go out without him
> J.L.B.: can't hardly speak english . . .
>
> R.A.: I am in heaven, man
> T.B.: and this is the way they talk
> J.H.: this is the voice
> S.A..: in touch with the voice
> J.L.B.: and this is the way they talk (104, 110)

(Certain words, especially profane ones, are rather mumbled and spelled as pronounced; the repeated refrain "eresanen" is someone saying "There's an end" quickly.) Ashley's (and sometimes other singers') phrases are actually the chant that had run underneath the four stories—just as, in *Now Eleanor's Idea*, "The Song" appeared backgrounded in act 2 only to be foregrounded in act 4.

Even more unusual, given the context, *Dust* ends with four of what Ashley aptly refers to as "quasi-country-music songs"—though he also notes that they are too long and too narrative to fit the popular genre.[11] Narratively speaking, these are supposed to be songs that No Legs heard on the radio in the hospital under the influence of morphine, into which he has substituted stories to make them make sense. In “Don’t Get Your Hopes Up,” Humbert sings the part of a housewife who regularly receives roses from a secret lover. Buckner, in “Just One More Time,” consoles an aging friend who, though happily married, wants to recapture some youth by falling in love one more time. La Barbara, in “It’s Easy,” plays a woman who enjoys seducing older men:

> My friends all think it’s strange.
> They speak psychology.
> I’ve stopped trying to explain
> What it means to me . . .
> I take one day off every week
> from the parties and the fun
> and I give it to somebody
> that doesn’t have anyone. (148–49)

Finally, Sam Ashley sings “The Angel of Loneliness,” about an aspiring country singer who “didn’t make it” but who is cheered up by a little old lady who tells him, “There’s nothing wrong with you / That a little love can’t fix.” This seems, ultimately, to be Ashley’s prescription for his fictional and yet nonfictional friends living across the street in Tribeca Park.

Celestial Excursions (2003)

Celestial Excursions is a marked departure from *Dust* and less personal-seeming than almost any of its predecessors. For one thing, the text contains a sonnet and a letter by Giordano Bruno—a rare instance of Ashley’s setting someone else’s words to music. This is also one of Ashley’s most elaborately musical operas; the third act (of three) affords Ashley himself long keyboard solos between the songs, over elaborate backgrounds developed by Ashley and Hamilton. The chorus (that is, the other singers relative to whoever is doing the main solo in any particular song) tends to sing in chords, and the chords are all within the C major scale. The bass note keeps changing, though (D, E, F, G, or A, and B at the very end, never a C), creating mostly minor seventh chords and sus chords, both types expectant sonorities that promise a resolution which never arrives. Also, Ashley expands here on his attempt in *Dust* to make the texts contrapuntal, so that to catch all the meaning one really does have to stream more than one line of text at a time.

Textually speaking, this is a complex opera, and unusual for Ashley in that the three acts are very different in structure, exhibiting less symmetry than usual. Old age is the general topic. “The fear,” poetizes Ashley in an introduction, is that we won't go gently or abruptly into that good night. We will hang on in the endurance trials of old age, forever rehearsing in the early morning twilight, fortified by a few hours of faulty sleep, the plot or why there is no plot, the explanations, the whys, the lists, the old grievances never to be settled now, the stories never told or passed on, the interruptions, the terrifying proportions, everything larger than it is known to be, distorted in the mirror, and again and again.[12]

In act 1, titled "Is It Light Yet?," he describes a series of songs rehearsed in the early morning, "trying to get the story right"; the premise of *That Morning Thing* comes back to mind. Act 2, "Asylum," is a dialogue among four old people at an assisted living facility, frequently interrupted by songs. And act 3, "The River Deepens," is a series of five reminiscences separated by instrumental interludes.

Ashley plays an old man named Dwayne—leftover from *Perfect Lives*, one supposes. A song titled "Characters" discusses the difference between so-called fictitious characters and so-called real ones, always a fine line in Ashley's operas. ("The real ones can pretend to be the real ones, of course. / This is called acting.")[13] One of his examples is a conductor leading an orchestra who, by his assumed authority, is pretending to be the composer. This is followed by a scene called "Alcohol," a lecture on the different types of alcoholism, relating it to hypoglycemia, the buildup of THIQ, which defines the classic alcoholic, and the self-defeating medication for depression. Next, in "Mr. or Ms. or Mrs. N," Sam describes the procedure of taking a patient from the "Death's Door Hospital" to the asylum named in act 2, an assisted-living facility, as the chorus sings a reminiscence about a country-and-western song from Ashley's youth called "Milk Cow Blues" by the Bob Wills Band. These separate streams, one couched in the present and one in the past, require some familiarity if one is to hear both at once.

The next two sections, "Love Letter" and "Bruno," are intertwined. One is about a love letter that a lonely lady has asked the narrator to write; the other contains the Giordano Bruno texts. The sonnet, in a translation by Bruno scholar Ingrid D. Rowland, is a magnificent love letter in itself:

O may I never come to rue the love
Without which I've no wish for happiness.
Though for its sake I sacrifice to prove
I've no wish not to wish for its largesse.
Whether the sky be bright, dark, chill, or hot,
The phoenix is but one and ever true;
No destiny or fate can breach the knot
That even death itself could not undo.[14]

The love letter is sung beneath the sonnet, thus affirming their equivalence. The following song, "Subaru," is not about the car (as the text informs us) but about a telescope in Hawaii developed in 1998 by the National Astronomical Observatory of Japan, which has made some important discoveries in the vicinity of the constellation Orion. Subaru is the Japanese term for the Pleiades. "Raoul" is a telling of a dream Ashley had about a man being shot in a dark forest. "Goodbye Walnut," the final scene, is about saying goodbye to an adopted American Indian daughter named Walnut, in a city with streets of deep water.

In act 2, "Asylum," an official of the asylum is accosted by characters who are seeking asylum from a "determination as if imposed from the outside." The basic texture and harmony of the act are interrupted by a series of songs, some of them very brief. (An E is played in the bass during the recurring sections of this act, a D during each of the songs.) Some of the songs are vignettes about the psychology of art making and, by extension, Ashley's view of it. For instance, "Depression Adaptation" is a theory about the connection of depression and creativity. The text in its entirety:

> Manic depression is an ancient adaptation to the rigors of prehistoric life.
> Manic, when it's time to hunt. Depressed, when it's time to hibernate.
> Hibernation is a time for dreams.
> Thus, depression is the mode of the imagination.
> Get it? (41–42)

"The Baguette" is a whimsy about Samuel Beckett's needing to have a baguette for breakfast in order to write in French—in other words, about how one's imagination is affected by external circumstances. "I Love That Stuff" is a perky celebration of materialism:

> Got a Japanese car made in Tennessee.
> Victoria's Secret is no secret to me.
> I love that stuff. I love that stuff . . .
>
> Hardly wait to get off work to see the latest styles.
> I know every shop in every mall in thirty miles.
> I love that stuff. (47–48)

And "It's Only Fun" is a disguised theory of creativity, its verses stating that something can only be fun, funny, poetry, or beautiful if it's against the law, that is, if it breaks through some barrier in our daily mindset.

Act 3, "The River Deepens," is a series of monologues broken by a refrain referring to old age: "The river deepens when it gets down to the sea, the river deepens." "Ozzie Smith" describes seeing the famous St. Louis Cardinals shortstop on television, with the refrain "The love was pouring down like rain." This is the story of Ozzie Smith, who has announced his retirement, playing in his last All-Star game. He is just in middle age, but he is old by baseball standards. (Ashley loves watching baseball on television late at night.) In "Therapy" Humbert describes being told rather dubiously in therapy that she must have been sexually abused by her father in childhood, just because she mourns his passing. Buckner, in "Nightmare," recounts a dream about a wild ride in a car whose steering ratio makes it difficult to steer. "Grandmother" is a true story about how Nick Bertoni's grandmother moved out of her house because she couldn't stand the noise of Ashley's practicing music next door; a year later a tornado destroyed the house, so Ashley's music had actually saved her life.

The final story, "Yes, I Know," is drawn from Ashley's teaching experiences at Mills College. Against his better judgment he accepted into a seminar class a Chinese woman who had always scared him. Also in the class was a woman interested in the Armenian-born spiritual teacher George Gurdjieff (ca. 1877–1949) and whose husband was an engineer. The class went beautifully, with wonderful discussions. At the semester's end, Ashley was sitting in a coffee shop alone. The fan of Gurdjieff joined him, and then the Chinese woman came by.

> She said how happy she was to have been accepted in the seminar.
> She said that before the seminar weeks she had been troubled for many years
> by a ghost that stayed near her left shoulder
> and prevented her from being accepted by other people
> and prevented her from doing her work.
> Then she said to the woman whose husband was an engineer (Sure!),
> "You took away the ghost."
> The woman said, "Yes, I know."
> I never saw the woman again.
> Higher education. (102)

Concrete (2006–9)

Ashley's most recently completed opera, *Concrete*, is perhaps his most conceptually simple; the theme of the opera is, in fact, "the secret lives of seemingly ordinary people." It also represents a departure from his usual ways of structuring time. Instead of planning out and notating beats, bars, and chord changes, Ashley wanted a more flexible structure that would allow the performers to use their own rhythm in the stories. Perhaps just as significant, this is the first opera in which Ashley did not include his own voice. Hamilton used the software program Ableton Live to set up loops of the "orchestras," the background sound material; for instance, one loop might run on a five-minute cycle, another on a seven-minute cycle, and so these sound loops, mixed live for each performance by Ashley, create a free continuum from which the singers choose the pitches they want, and over which they perform at their own rate. Given that program, Ashley performs (or composes, in real time) the orchestras directly in Ableton Live from the back of the hall.

Concrete was originally staged live as a card game in which the singers seemingly played cards during the four ensemble scenes, called "Meditations" (these cards actually contain the text from which they are singing). In the course of the work five autobiographical stories were told: the first four by Humbert, Buckner, La Barbara, and Sam Ashley, respectively, the fifth *in serie* by the entire cast. This version is documented on the Lovely Music recording. In 2009, however, Ashley became dissatisfied with the sense of disconnection among the five stories, and he rewrote the opera. He added some textual material and divided the piece into twelve stories, interlaced with some solo meditations by the old man called "The Observer," who is the central character. Each story can now be sung by any of the singers, and there are now pitch cues embedded in the prerecorded orchestra mix.

In any case, the lines in *Concrete*'s "Meditations" are each seven syllables long and are to be accentuated in the same rhythm and pattern as the phrase, "*Take* time / to *think* it over." On the recording, each of the stories is preceded by a brief prelude in which thoughts spin around among the five singers. "The old man lives in concrete" is a recurring refrain, which refers to Ashley living in the concrete jungle of New York City, though as the text says, "What is concrete, complaint? / Wouldn't live anywhere else."[15] The first story, "Ideas About Thinking," sung by Humbert, is a saga about a woman friend of Ashley's who started as a champion golfer, studied ceramics, opened a boutique selling clothes she designed, hired an important friend to deal with four girls who are shoplifting from her, gave up the store and moved to Canada, had international adventures buying cocaine, got thrown out of Canada, moved to Hawaii and married a sailor, miraculously survived an ocean disaster in which he was killed, and now lives on a small island.

Like Buckner's story in *Dust*, two stories come from Ashley's army years in Texas. In "Insatiable Desire," sung by Buckner, he is friends with an accomplished cheating gambler, whom he rescues from a high-stakes poker game in which he could have been killed for winning too much. Later the friend barely and courageously manages to avoid a high-speed collision with another car. The high-stakes gambler friend eventually becomes an airline pilot. Years later, on a flight from Europe, the friend is announced as the pilot, and Ashley shares a Coke with him. "Interchangeability," narrated by La Barbara, tells of a different friend, a talented clarinetist, who starts out wanting to get a Ph.D. as a Joseph Conrad scholar but ends by becoming a horse-race gambler. A side story expresses sympathy for a fellow band member, a saxophonist, who falls in love with a woman who turns out to be a man. Actual tips for playing the horses are included in the story.

Sam Ashley's story, "A Day on Planet Gilbert," is the most elaborate and disturbing. The narrator tells a story of a friend who has trouble making a living, first in the Detroit DJ scene and later as a diamond dealer, both times because of organized crime. The friend likes to call Ashley on the phone, and in one phone call asks him to come visit. But Ashley is about to go on tour—not knowing that the friend is hoping Ashley will visit because he has cancer, and time is short. While in Rome, Ashley is sleeping in an apartment at the American Academy, and in the middle of the night his blanket is suddenly forcibly pulled off. He turns on the light, and can't find a cause. Upon returning to New York, he gets a call from the friend's wife and determines that the moment of his death was exactly the moment his blanket was pulled off. "I can't explain this to myself in any way." The most poignant moment follows a recitation of the friend's flights from various organized criminals:

> The only conversation I remember
> Comes from my complaining
> About the difficulties
> Of having my work in music produced.
> He says, "But you have made an ideal life.
> You can do anything you want to do
> And nobody can hurt you."
>
> This is an important lesson for me.
> I never complain again,
> Even to myself.[16]

In 2005, when the Ensemble MAE asked Ashley for a five-minute composition, he arranged a shorter version of the first story of *Concrete*, "Ideas About Thinking," into a piece called *Hidden Similarities*. He wanted them to read the story in their native Dutch, and he arranged for the text to be passed around among the performers, who take turns coming to the microphones as the others play sounds "peculiar to their instruments." Ensemble MAE released a charming recording of the piece in 2005.

Quicksand and Beyond

As this book was in preparation, Ashley was working on yet another opera, which he said will be his longest and most ambitious ever: *Quicksand*. It's a shoot-'em-up spy thriller written in the form of a novel and paying homage to the hard-bitten styles of Elmore Leonard and John Le Carré, with a protagonist who accidentally gets involved in the overthrow of a small southeast Asian country. It's inspired by, and clearly loosely based on, a trip Ashley took to Thailand with Mimi's yoga group. The text, published as a novel by Burning Books in 2011, is an entertaining read, shifting back and forth across the line between autobiography and wild imagination. At age eighty, he works on the opera constantly, and with the same boundless enthusiasm I've observed in him for thirty years.

I am painfully aware how inadequate this book is for doing justice to Ashley's music—at best, it can be an incitement for listeners to begin exploring it for themselves. His recorded operas alone last over sixteen hours, in addition to all the spin-off pieces, ONCE festival works, unrecorded operas, and much else. He possesses a huge audio archive waiting to be made public someday. He has been phenomenally prolific, and his work is dense with text and unconventional techniques. The literature alluded to in his works would fill a bookcase. There are many textual hints to elaborate, many performance practices to clarify, many structures to re-create. (Again, some of the musical techniques are detailed on my website at http://www.kylegann.com/Ashley.html.) Like Charles Ives, Ashley has left enough for the musicologists to wrangle with for generations.

As noted in chapter 4, Philip Glass's *Einstein on the Beach* (1976) sparked a new mania for opera reconceptualized along minimalist lines. Glass's subsequent operas—the most popular being *Satyagraha* (1980), *Akhnaten* (1982), and *The Voyage* (1992)—along with those of John Adams (*Nixon in China* [1987] and *The Death of Klinghoffer* [1991]) and others have once again made opera a popular, timely, and feasible genre. They have also, if gradually at first, had the effect of returning to a more conventional notion of stage opera, with arias sung by singers acting in costume onstage and accompanied by a conventional orchestra in the pit. Surprisingly (for those of us who lived through the transformation), conventional opera has made a comeback.

This leaves Ashley somewhat out on a limb. Others have applied electronic technology to opera (Tod Machover's 1987 science-fiction opera *Valis* is notable), but hardly anyone has followed Ashley's lead of revamping the idea of opera with an eye toward mass media such as television. His most visible successor in this arena is Mikel Rouse (b. 1957), whose *Dennis Cleveland* (1995), *The End of Cinematics* (1997), *Funding* (2001), and other theater works have incorporated film and live television to greatly update the genre's cultural relevance, and who acknowledges a deep debt to Ashley as inspiration and predecessor. Ashley remains the one major composer who has envisioned a new future for opera, its reincarnation into a world of mass media rather than in an opera-house tradition sometimes seen as perhaps moribund even by its promoters. For Ashley's fans, those other operas (except for Rouse's and Machover's) seem like an optimistic, possibly short-lived attempt to reinvigorate an older form. At some point, opera in its original sense—a collusion of music, text, and image—will be forced into rebirth in a new, digital, computerized, multidimensional world. When that happens, we have only Ashley to look back to for cues as to the next step.

There are, after all, pleasures in Ashley's operas that those new stage operas can never provide. One is the counterpoint between the greater aural accessibility of the text—vernacular phrases sung in natural speech rhythms—and the multilayered ambiguity of the references, or in the voices keeping up two or more continuities at once. Another is the trance-inducing repetitiveness of Ashley's backgrounds, the shimmering chords, the ostinatos, the rhythmically off-kilter chord progressions. The third, in the completed video for *Perfect Lives*, is the counterpoint between image and text, the fact that the words may describe one thing, while the camera shows us something else, as our brains struggle to fit everything together. Plus, Ashley's music often has a pop or boogie-woogie surface that can reel in listeners who find even new conventional operas too stodgy. An opera onstage, with a plot, is bound to remain a fairly linear experience; Ashley's operas give us so many streams to follow at once that each listening can be a fairly different adventure. It would be difficult to argue, I think, that any other composer has come up with and fully explored so new a paradigm for opera, nor one so attuned to our postmodern and polytextual age.

"The Bar" from *Perfect Lives* ends with a meditation on the place (or lack of place) of art in a corporate world:

> Television is neither true nor false.
> It's industry. . . .
> Television made without industry . . .
> Alone, in a word . . .
> Can cause a sinking feeling.
> There can be a loss of trust. . . .

> Everybody works to be a part of industry.
> To be a part of industry is to be real. . . .
> If you're a part of industry, both in your
> Industriousness and in the nature of your work,
> There is a chance that everybody will like your work,
> Because it is part of industry.
> And things that are not a part of industry
> Are not possible to like.
> Likeability is less important than
> Recognition by the industry. . . .
> 'N that's a reason to be serious.[17]

This is a clever play on the dual meaning of *industry*, meaning continuous work, on one hand—and Ashley has never lacked for industriousness—and the corporate regimentation of distribution and taste on the other. Ashley's music is not "part of industry" in the latter sense. It is excluded from the world of American television and mass media, just as it is marginalized by the classical music establishment. It is a tribute to his originality that his music has never been mainstreamed during his lifetime. He is still one of the great outsider composers, all the more extreme in that respect in that he dared try to break into television, a mass medium that almost no other recent composer would have even attempted.

All the same, Ashley has performed his music around the world, and it has been loved around the world. The tribute to the attractiveness, the rightness of his vision is that even without "recognition by the industry" it has garnered such a diverse and devoted following. It may take us decades to figure out everything he's saying, but the attempt itself is already an inspiration.

CHRONOLOGICAL LIST OF WORKS BY ROBERT ASHLEY

Robert Ashley occasionally retitles previously composed pieces, and the same title sometimes appears in different ways in different sources, so there may not be exact correspondence between a work found on a sound recording and a piece found in this list or online references.

1957	Film music for George Manupelli's *The Image in Time*
1957	*The Fox* for voice and tape
1959/1979	*Piano Sonata (Christopher Columbus Crosses to the New World in the Niña, the Pinta and the Santa Maria Using Only Dead Reckoning and a Crude Astrolabe)* for piano
1960	Film music for George Manupelli's *The Bottleman*
1960	*The Fourth of July* for electronic tape
1961	Film music for George Manupelli's *The House*
1961	*Maneuvers for Small Hands* for piano
1961	*Public Opinion Descends upon the Demonstrators*, electronic music theater
1961	*Something for Clarinet . . .* for clarinet or flute, pianos, and tape
1962	*Complete with Heat* for orchestral instruments and tape
1962	*Details for Two Pianists, IIb* for one piano, four hands
1962	*Detroit Divided* for four-channel tape
1962	*Fives* for 2 pianos, 2 percussionists, and string quintet
1963	*Boxing*, for sound-producing dance
1963	*in memoriam . . . ESTEBAN GOMEZ (quartet)* for four players
1963	*in memoriam . . . JOHN SMITH (concerto)* for three players and assistants

1963	*in memoriam . . . CRAZY HORSE (symphony)* for twenty or more wind or string or other sustaining instruments
1963	*in memoriam . . . KIT CARSON (opera)* for eight-part ensemble
1963	*Trios (White on White)* for open instrumentation
1964	*Big Danger in Five Parts* for electronic tape
1964	*Combination Wedding and Funeral* for electronic music theater
1964	Film music for George Manupelli's *Jenny and the Poet*
1964	*Interludes for the Space Theater* for sound-producing dance
1964	*Kittyhawk (An Antigravity Piece)* for electronic music theater
1964	*The Lecture Series* (alternate title: *Joyroad Interchange*) for electronic music theater, co-composed with Mary Ashley
1964	*The Wolfman* for amplified voice and *The Wolfman Tape*
1964	*The Wolfman Tape* for magnetic tape
1965	*The Entrance* for two-keyboard electronic organ
1965	Film music for George Manupelli's *My May*
1965	*Orange Dessert* for electronic music theater
1965	*Unmarked Interchange* for electronic music theater, co-composed with the ONCE Group
1965	*Untitled Mixes* for tape, co-composed with the Bob James Trio
1965–78	*Waiting Room* (alternate title: *Quartet*) for any number of wind or string instruments
1966	*Night Train* for electronic music theater, co-composed with Mary Ashley
1967	*Frogs*, from *That Morning Thing*
1967	*She Was a Visitor*, from *That Morning Thing*, for speaker and chorus
1967	*That Morning Thing*, opera for five principal voices, eight dancers, women's chorus, and tape
1968	Film music for George Manupelli's *Overdrive*
1968	*Purposeful Lady Slow Afternoon*, from *Wolfman Motorcity Revue*, for electronic music theater
1968	*Trial of Anne Opie Wehrer and Unknown Accomplices for Crimes Against Humanity* for electronic music theater
1968	*The Wolfman Motorcity Revue* for electronic music theater
1969	Film music for George Manupelli's *Portraits, Self-Portraits, and Still Lifes*
1969–71	Sound Tracks to George Manupelli's *Dr. Chicago* films

1970	*Fancy Free* or *It's There* for speaker and cassette machines
1970	Film music for Philip Makanna's *Battery Davis*
1970	*Illusion Models*, hypothetical computer tasks
1970	*Morton Feldman Says* for sound-producing dance
1972	*In Sara, Mencken, Christ and Beethoven There Were Men and Women* for voice and electronics
1972	*String Quartet Describing the Motions of Large Real Bodies* for string quartet with electronics
1973	*Revised, Finally (April 1961–April 1973) for Gordon Mumma* for pairs of bell-like instruments
1974	*How Can I Tell the Difference?* for violin or viola with electronics and tape
1975	*Night Sport* for improvising voice and various distractions
1975	*Over the Telephone*, remote control of a performance in another place
1976	*Music with Roots in the Aether*, television opera
1976	*Title Withdrawn*, music theater on videotape
1976	*What She Thinks*, music theater on videotape
1979–80	*Perfect Lives*, opera for television
1979	*Automatic Writing* for voice, electronic instruments, and special recording techniques
1979	*Ideas from the Church* for voice and tape
1981	*The Lessons*, television opera
1981	*Music Word Fire and I Would Do It Again Coo Coo: The Lessons* for voices and electronic instruments
1982–87	*Atalanta (Acts of God)*, three operas composed to be intermingled
1982	*Tap Dancing in the Sand* for solo voice
1984	*Atalanta Strategy*, television opera
1985	*Improvement: Don Leaves Linda*, opera for solo voices, chorus, orchestra, and electronics
1985	*Odalisque* for solo voice, orchestra (24 instruments), and chorus
1987	*eL/Aficionado*, opera for solo voices, chorus, solo piano, and electronics
1988	*Basic 10* for snare drum or other percussion
1988	*Problems in the Flying Saucer* for two solo voices
1988	*Superior Seven* for flute with orchestral instruments and chorus
1990	*Yellow Man with Heart with Wings* for tape

1991 *Empire (The History of Tomato Soup)*, from the opera *Atalanta (Acts of God)*, for voice and tape or piano

1991 *The Max Anecdote*, from the opera *Atalanta (Acts of God)*, for voice and tape or piano

1991 *The Offering of Images*, from the opera *Improvement (Don Leaves Linda)*, for baritone voice and piano

1991 *Outcome Inevitable* for chamber orchestra of 8 or more

1991 *The Producer Speaks*, from the opera *Atalanta (Acts of God)*, for baritone voice and piano

1992 *The Song*, from the opera *Now Eleanor's Idea*, for solo voice, chorus voices, and pre-recorded electronic orchestra

1992 *Tract* for voice with pre-recorded orchestra and optional string trio

1992 *Van Cao's Meditation* for piano

1993 *Factory Preset* for tape

1993 *The Immortality Songs: Love Is a Good Example*, for voice

1993 *Now Eleanor's Idea*, opera for solo voices and pre-recorded orchestra

1994 *Foreign Experiences*, opera for solo voices, chorus, and pre-recorded orchestra

1997 *Balseros*, opera for solo voices, chorus, and pre-recorded orchestra, with libretto by Maria Irene Fornes

1997 *When Famous Last Words Fail You* for voice, chorus, and orchestra

1998 *Dust*, opera for solo voices and pre-recorded orchestra

1998 *Your Money My Life Goodbye* for solo voices and pre-recorded orchestra

2003 *Celestial Excursions*, opera for solo voices and pre-recorded orchestra

2004 *Tap Dancing in the Sand* for speaker, alto voice, and 8 instruments

2005 *Hidden Similarities* for voices and 8 instruments

2006 *Concrete*, opera for solo voices and pre-recorded orchestra

2011– *Quicksand*, opera for solo voice, chorus, pre-recorded orchestra, and electronics

NOTES

Preface

1. Cope, *New Directions in Music*, 111.

2. Sleeve for *Purposeful Lady Slow Afternoon*, on *Electronic Sound*, Mainstream MS-5010 (LP recording), 1971, n.p.

3. Ibid.

Chapter One. "Oh, How We Misunderstand"

1. Gann, "Shouting at the Dead." 89.

2. Sabatini, "Mikhail Bakhtin," 187.

3. Robert Ashley, interview with Steve Smith, quoted in his blog "Night After Night," http://www.nightafternight.com/night_after_night/2005/10/private_lives_m.html, accessed July 10, 2009.

4. Ashley, *Perfect Lives*, 186.

5. "Blue" Gene Tyranny, interview with the author, New York City, November 29, 2010.

Chapter Two. "The Vessel of the Eternal Present"

1. http://www.aadl.org/moaa/pictorial_history/1900–1919pg1#Milling, accessed July 8, 2011.

2. http://www.aadl.org/moaa/pictorial_history/1930–1939pg2, accessed July 8, 2011.

3. No death certificate for Alvah J. Ashley the elder is available, but the city directory for 1909 is the first to list Sarah as a widow.

4. The dates are from Nancy Reynolds's obituary; neither she nor any relatives are listed in the city directory, however, before 1930. Other information is from Anne Ward Ashley Conlon and her husband Pat, interviewed in August 2010.

5. Libretto printed in the liner notes to Robert Ashley's *Foreign Experiences*, Lovely Music CD 1008 (2006), 57–58.

6. Phone communication with Theodore Hariton, June 12, 2011.

7. Ashley, *Perfect Lives*, 39.

8. Obituary in the *Ann Arbor News*, April 27, 1950.

9. Ibid.

10. Robert Ashley, interview with the author, New York City, June 9, 2009. Further unnoted quotations are taken from a series of interviews conducted at Ashley's loft in New York from June 2009 to August 2010.

11. Robert Ashley, "Foreword," in Ashley, *Music with Roots in the Aether*, 9.

12. Ashley, *Perfect Lives*, 74–77.

13. Sumner, Burch, and Sumner, *Guests Go in to Supper*, 100.

14. Robert Ashley, liner notes to *Dust* (Lovely Music CD 1006, 2000), 22, 24.

15. Ibid., 36–38.

16. Flower, *Downstairs, Upstairs*, 47.

17. Finney, *Profile of a Lifetime*, 115–40.

18. Lester Trimble, liner notes to *Finney/Weiss Chamber Works*, CRI SD116; http://www.dramonline.org/albums/finney-weiss-chamber-works/notes, accessed July 16, 2010; see also Edith Borroff. "Finney, Ross Lee." In *Grove Music Online*. Oxford Music Online, http://www.oxfordmusiconline.com/subscriber/article/grove/music/09683, accessed May 6, 2012.

19. Finney, *Profile of a Lifetime*, 159–60.

20. "Hans David Dead; Musicologist, 65; Professor at the University of Michigan and Author," *New York Times*, October 31, 1967.

21. Mendel, "Hans T. David," 407.

22. "*Mary Baldwin College Bluestocking*, 1935," vol. 12 (1935), at http://www.archive.org/stream/marybaldwincolle1935mary/marybaldwincolle1935mary_djvu.txt, accessed July 27, 2010; see also the *Mary Baldwin Bulletin*, vol. 6, no, 3 (March 1935) at http://www.archive.org/stream/marybaldwinbulle1935mary/marybaldwinbulle1935mary_djvu.txt, accessed July 27, 2010.

23. Stephen Spackman. "Riegger, Wallingford." In *Grove Music Online*. Oxford Music Online, http://www.oxfordmusiconline.com/subscriber/article/grove/music/23432, accessed May 8, 2012.

24. Miller, "ONCE and Again," 16.

25. Ibid.

26. Robert Ashley, libretto in the liner notes to *Dust* (Lovely Music CD 1006), 83–84.

27. Miller, "ONCE and Again," 23.

28. Ibid., 22.

29. Finney, *Profile of a Lifetime*, 161. Finney mentions Ashley several times during a brief, faintly sympathetic account of the ONCE festivals, remarking that Ashley "was very eager to establish a new kind of theater at the University" and that he later "moved more and more into the theatrical concept of performance" (170–71).

30. Miller, "ONCE and Again," 17.

31. Ibid., 22–23.

32. James, "ONCE," 363–67.

33. Finney, *Profile of a Lifetime*, 173.

34. Malcolm MacDonald. "Gerhard, Roberto." In *Grove Music Online*. Oxford Music Online, http://www.oxfordmusiconline.com/subscriber/article/grove/music/10920, accessed May 6, 2012.

35. Ibid.

36. Bernard Benoliel, liner notes to *Gerhard: SymphonynNo. 3*, Collages / *Epithalamion / Piano Concerto*, Chandos CHAN 9556, 1997.

37. Miller, "ONCE and Again," 28.

38. Ibid., 34, 36.

39. Ibid., 18.

40. James, "ONCE," 370.

Chapter Three. "When Slow Starts to Mean Something, We Crave Fast"

1. "Letter from Robert Ashley, 2006," in the booklet accompanying *Dr. Chicago: A Film Trilogy*, dir. George Manupelli (George Manupelli Films, 2006), 8.

2. Rancont, "Coins, Balloons and Explosions."

3. Robert Ashley, interview with the author, New York City, June 10, 2009. Further unnoted quotations are taken from a series of interviews conducted at Ashley's loft in New York City from June 2009 to August 2010.

4. Gann, "Shouting at the Dead," 89–90.

5. Hanhardt, "Chance in a Lifetime."

6. Cage, *Notations*, n.p.

7. Nyman, *Experimental Music*, 10.

8. Ashley, *Sonata*, n.p.

9. "Performance History," http://www.robertashley.org/, accessed July 20, 2009.

10. Roger Reynolds, "ONCE then . . . what was needed," liner notes to *Music from the ONCE Festival, 1961–1966*, New World Records 80567-2 (2003), 122.

11. "Anne Wehrer," obituary in the *San Francisco Chronicle*, March 25, 2007, http://www.sfgate.com/cgi-bin/article.cgi?f=/c/a/2007/03/25/MNWEHRERAN50.DTL, accessed July 20, 2009.

12. Miller, "ONCE and Again," 36–37.

13. These and other facts are taken from ibid., 41–49.

14. James, "ONCE," 371.

15. "Blue" Gene Tyranny, interview with the author, New York City, November 29, 2010.

16. Miller, "ONCE and Again," 103–4.

17. The composer Samuel Vriezen has come up with a hypothetical algorithm for the way Ashley arrived at these numbers. One multiplies each successive number by 7 and subtracts one more than the number before last to get the next:

1 × 7 = 7;	7 – 1 = 6 [max. no. of people in version 1]
6 × 7 = 42;	42 – (1 + 1) = 40 [max. in version 2]
40 × 7 = 280;	280 – (6 + 1) = 273 [version 3]
273 × 7 = 1,911;	911 – (40 + 1) = 1,870
1870 × 7 = 13,090;	13,090 – (273 + 1) = 12,816 [version 4]
12816 × 7 = 89,712;	89,712 – (1,870 + 1) = 87,841
87841 × 7 = 614,887;	614,887 – (12,816 + 1) = 602,070
602070 × 7 = 4,214,490;	4,214,490 – (87,841 + 1) = 4,126,648
4126648 × 7 = 28,886,536;	28,886,536 – (602,070 + 1) = 28,284,465

This result misses the maximum for Version 5 by 6000. Vriezen speculates that Ashley did the multiplication by hand and mistook 28886536 for 28880536, taking the first 6 for a 0.

18. Hitchcock, "Current Chronicle," 246.

19. Robert Ashley, "Public Opinion Decends upon the Demonstrators," in Ashley, *Outside of Time*, 568.

20. Vigneras, "The Cartographer Diogo Ribeiro," 78.

21. "Composers' Notes: Robert Ashley," in liner notes to *Music from the ONCE Festival, 1961–1966*, New World Records 0567-2 (2003), 112.

22. Robert Ashley, "Robert Ashley" in *Source* no. 1 (1967), 45.

23. "Blue" Gene Tyranny, interview with the author, Brooklyn, New York, November 29, 2010.

24. Ashley, Austin, and Stockhausen, "Conversation," 106.

25. This same recording was released on *Music from the ONCE Festival, 1961–1966*, on New World Records, in 2003.

26. Untitled and unsigned review in *Anuario* 3 (1967), 133.

27. "Composer's Notes," 111.

28. Robert Ashley, liner notes to *The Wolfman*, Plana-A 20NMN.048 (2002), n.p.

29. Ibid.

30. Ibid.

31. Ibid.

32. Johnson, *Scores*, 151.

33. Ibid., 123.

34. Ibid., 31–32.

35. http://www.johncage.info/cdlabels/odyssey32160156.html, accessed June 19, 2010.

36. Robert Ashley, liner notes to *Automatic Writing*, Lovely Music LCD 1002 (1996).

37. Robert Ashley, "*Fancy Free or It's There*," *Soundings* no. 1 (January 1972): 45–50.

38. Miller, "ONCE and Again" 80, 82; James, "ONCE," 381.

39. Ibid., 383–84; Robert Ashley, *Kittyhawk (An Anti-Gravity Piece)*, in Ashley, *Outside of Time*, 410, 412.

40. James, "ONCE," 386.

41. Ibid., 387.

42. "Letter from Robert Ashley," 7.

Chapter 4. "Incredibly Slowly Our View Begins to Slide"

1. Jeremy Drake. "Milhaud, Darius." In Grove Music Online. Oxford Music Online, http://www.oxfordmusiconline.com/subscriber/article/grove/music/18674, accessed May 6, 2012.

2. Robert Ashley, "The Most Difficult Job in the World: Teaching at Mills College," in Ashley, *Outside of Time*, 316.

3. This information is courtesy of Karma Pippin, assistant archivist, F. W. Olin Library, Mills College.

4. Gluck, "Shiraz Arts Festival," 20–28, 200.

5. Keith Waldrop, "John Barton Wolgamot," in liner notes to Robert Ashley, *In Sara, Mencken, Christ and Beethoven There Were Men and Women*, Lovely Music CD 4921 (2002), 13.

6. Robert Ashley, "John Barton Wolgamot," in liner notes to Robert Ashley, *In Sara, Mencken, Christ and Beethoven There Were Men and Women*, Lovely Music CD 4921 (2002), 39.

7. Ashley, *Music with Roots in the Aether*, 20.

8. Ashley, "Automatic Writing," in Ashley, *Outside of Time*, 590.

9. Robert Ashley, interview with the author, New York City, June 10, 2009.

Chapter 5. "I'm Not the Same Person That I Used to Be"

1. Robert Ashley, "Speech as Music," in Ashley, *Outside of Time*, 76, 78.

2. Robert Ashley, "A New Kind of Opera," in Ashley, *Outside of Time*, 136.

3. Robert Ashley, "The Future of Music," lecture delivered at the University of California at San Diego, April 15, 2000, typescript, 9.

4. Ashley, "Speech as Music," 76.

5. Robert Ashley, liner notes to *eL/Aficionado*, Lovely Music CD 1004 (1994)), n.p.

6. "Robert Ashley," in Sumner, Burch, and Sumner, *Guests Go in to Supper*, 106–7.

7. Holm-Hudson, "Music, Text, and Image," 51. Actually, the original intention was for 28-minute episodes. Holm-Hudson details some respects in which Ashley's initial structure was squeezed down into the 24:40 format, with some resulting non-synchronization between text and beat pattern.

8. Ashley, *Perfect Lives*, 162–63.

9. Holm-Hudson, "Music, Text and Image," 86–91, 255.

10. Lama Anagarika Govinda, "Introductory Foreword," in Evans-Wentz, *Tibetan Book of the Dead*, liv–lix.

11. Ibid., lxii.

12. Gann, "Shouting at the Dead," 89.

13. All excerpts are from Ashley, *Perfect Lives.* Page references follow the excerpts.

14. Ashley, afterword to *Atalanta*, 190–91.

15. Ibid., 122.

16. In the 1991 publication of *Perfect Lives*, Ashley gives this rhythmic template as alternating between five-beat and six-beat triplet phrases, but this is an error.

17. Ashley, *Perfect Lives*, 136.

18. Holm-Hudson, "Music, Text, and Image,"59–61.

Chapter 6. "Who Could Speak If Every Word Had Meaning?"

1. Thomas Buckner, interview with the author, New York City, July 25, 2009.

2. "Atalanta." *Encyclopædia Britannica Online*: http://search.eb.com/eb/article-9010029, accessed August 9, 2009.

3. Robert Ashley, afterword to *Atalanta*, 202.

4. Robert Ashley, "The Future of Music," lecture delivered at the University of California at San Diego, April 15, 2000, typescript, 9.

5. Ashley, *Atalanta*, 17. Further page references follow the excerpts. Sometimes there are discrepancies between the book and the libretto published with the recording; I have resolved them in favor of the earlier recording.

6. Robert Ashley, liner notes to *Atalanta (Acts of God) II*, Lovely Music LCD 3303-4 (2010), n.p.

Chapter 7. "If You Have to Ask You Can't Afford One"

1. Sumner, Burch, and Sumner, *Guests Go in to Supper*, 109.

2. David, "Bach's 'Musical Offering,'" 325.

3. Joan La Barbara, interview with the author, August 5, 2009; Tom Hamilton, interview with the author, New York City, July 22, 2009.

4. Unless noted otherwise, all excerpts from *Improvement* are from the libretto published with the recording, Elektra Nonesuch 79289-2 (1992), which is unpaginated.

5. Sumner, Burch, and Sumner, *Guests Go in to Supper*, 132–33.

6. Robert Ashley, interview with the author, New York City, July 28, 2010.

7. Michael Dobbs, "Ford and GM Scrutinized for Alleged Nazi Collaboration," *Washington Post*, November 30, 1998, http://www.washingtonpost.com/wp-srv/national/daily/nov98/nazicars30.htm, accessed August 24, 2010.

8. Excerpts from *eL/Aficionado* are from the libretto published with the liner notes of the recording, Lovely Music LCD 1004 (1994), which are unpaginated.

9. Excerpts are from the libretto in the liner notes to *Foreign Experiences*, Lovely Music LCD 1008 (2006). Page references follow the excerpts.

10. "Castaneda, Carlos." *Britannica Book of the Year, 1999. Encyclopædia Britannica Online.* http://search.eb.com/eb/article-9123827, accessed July 13, 2010.

11. Liner notes to *Foreign Experiences*, 4.

12. Ibid., 5.

13. Ibid., 8

14. See Bright, "'Heart Like a Car,'" which describes and includes of photo of Ashley's friend Dennis Martinez.

15. Ibid., 606, n. 9.

16. Libretto in the liner notes to *Now Eleanor's Idea*, Lovely Music LCD 1009 (2007), 27–28. Futher page references appear in the text.

17. Mark Aranovsky, *Simfonicheskiye iskaniya* [Symphonic explorations] (Leningrad: Sovetskiy kompozitor, 1979), quoted in Fanning, "Carl Nielsen," 13.

Chapter 8. "One Thing Follows the Next and I Just Do It"

1. The entire list is given in Ashley, "Immortality Songs," in Ashley, *Outside of Time*, 304–8.

2. Liner notes to *eL/Aficionado*, Lovely Music CD 1004 (1994), n.p.

3. Robert Ashley, "When Famous Last Words Fail You," typescript, 1997, 30–31.

4. Text in the liner notes to *Tap Dancing in the Sand*, Unsounds 15U (2007), 9–10.

5. E. J. Dionne Jr., "Italy Says It Found Cyanide in Sindona," *New York Times*, March 22,

1986, http://www.nytimes.com/1986/03/22/world/italy-says-it-found-cyanide-in-sindona.html?scp=1&sq=Sindona&st=cse, accessed August 23, 2010. Some lines in the opera are taken almost verbatim from this article.

6. Liner notes to *Your Money My Life Goodbye*, Lovely Music LCD 1005 (1999).

7. Robert Ashley, *Your Money My Life Goodbye*, typescript libretto (1998), lines 218–22, p. 6.

8. Excerpts from *Dust* are from the libretto in the liner notes to *Dust*, Lovely Music CD 1006 (2000). Page references are in the text.

9. Robert Ashley, "A Wonderful Jungle Full of Exotic Things," in Ashley, *Outside of Time*, 296, 298.

10. "'Everyone Knows Exactly What to Do,'" in Ashley, *Outside of Time*, 182–84.

11. Ibid., 182, 184.

12. Ashley, liner notes to *Celestial Excursions*, Lovely Music CD 1007 (2005), 4.

13. Libretto in the liner notes to *Celestial Excursions*, 12. Further page references to the libretto follow the excerpts.

14. Rowland, *From Heaven to Arcadia*, 260. Ashley had found it in the original article in the *New York Review of Books*, June 15, 2000.

15. Libretto in the liner notes to *Concrete*, Lovely Music CD 1010 (2008), 9.

16. Ibid., 85.

17. Ashley, *Perfect Lives*, 84–85. Some of the ellipses are in the original; others mark interruptions by the chorus.

SELECTED BIBLIOGRAPHY

Ashley, Robert. *Atalanta (Acts of God)*. Santa Fe: Burning Books, 2011.

———. *Music with Roots in the Aether*. Köln: MusikTexte, 2000.

———. *Outside of Time: Ideas about Music*. Köln: MusikTexte, 2009.

———. *Perfect Lives*. San Francisco: Burning Books/Archer Fields, 1991.

———. *Quicksand*. Santa Fe: Burning Books, 2011.

———. *Sonata*. New York: Sonic Art Editions, 1990.

Ashley, Robert, Larry Austin, and Karlheinz Stockhausen. "Conversation." *Source* 1 (1967): 106.

Austin, Larry, Douglas Kahn, and Nilendra Gurusinghe, eds. *Source: Music of the Avant-garde, 1966–1973*. Berkeley: University of California Press, 2011.

Bright, Brenda. "'Heart Like a Car': Hispano/Chicano Culture in Northern New Mexico." *American Ethnlogist* 25, no. 4 (November 1998): 583–609.

Cage, John. *Notations*. West Glover, Vt.: Something Else, 1969.

Castaneda, Carlos. *Journey to Ixtlan: The Lessons of Don Juan*. New York: Washington Square, 1972.

———. *A Separate Reality*. New York: Washington Square, 1971.

———. *The Teachings of Don Juan: A Yaqui Way of Knowledge*. Berkeley: University of California Press, 1972.

Cope, David. *New Directions in Music*. Dubuque: Brown, 1973.

David, Hans T. "Bach's 'Musical Offering.'" *Musical Quarterly* 23, no. 3 (July 1937): 314–32.

Evans-Wentz, W. Y., trans. *The Tibetan Book of the Dead*. London: Oxford University Press, 1960.

Fanning, David. "Carl Nielsen and Theories of Symphonism." In *Carl Nielsen Studies*, ed. Niels Krabbe, 4:9–25. Copenhagen: Ashgate, 2009.

Finney, Ross Lee. *Profile of a Lifetime: A Musical Autobiography*. New York: Peters, 1992.

Flower, John A. *Downstairs, Upstairs: The Changed Spirit and Face of College Life in America*. Akron: University of Akron Press, 2003.

Gagne, Cole, and Tracy Caras. *Soundpieces: Interviews with American Composers*. Metuchen, N.J.: Scarecrow, 1982.

Gann, Kyle. "The British Don't Have Oral Sex." *Village Voice* 39, no. 50 (December 13, 1994), 92.

———. "Finnegans Opera." *Village Voice* 36, no. 44 (October 29, 1991), 90.

———. "Opera Rad." *Village Voice* 44, no. 13 (April 4, 2000), 116, 119.

———. "Real-Life Ring." *Village Voice* 39, no 46 (November 15, 1994), 84.

———. "Shouting at the Dead." *Village Voice* 36, no. 41 (October 8, 1991), 89.

———. "Where the River Ends." *Village Voice* 48, no. 17 (April 29, 2003), 109.

Gluck, Robert. "The Shiraz Arts Festival: Western Avant-Garde Arts in 1970s Iran." *Leonardo* 40, no. 1 (2007): 20–28, 200.

Greenaway, Peter. *Four American Composers: A Series of One Hour Films about Robert Ashley, John Cage, Philip Glass and Meredith Monk*. Transatlantic Films (London)/Mystic Fire Video (New York), 1982–91 (film).

Hanhardt, John G. "Chance in a Lifetime: John G. Hanhardt on Nam June Paik." *ArtForum International* (April 2006), http://www.thefreelibrary.com/Chance+in+a+lifetime%3a+John+G.+Hanhardt+on+Nam+June+Paik.-a0144705008, accessed June 13, 2011.

Hitchcock, H. Wiley. "Current Chronicle." *Musical Quarterly* 48, no. 2 (April 1962): 246.

Holm-Hudson, Kevin James. "Music, Text, and Image in Robert Ashley's Video Opera *Perfect Lives*." Ph.D. diss., University of Illinois, 1992.

James, Richard S. "ONCE: Microcosm of the 1960s Musical and Multimedia Avant-Garde." *American Music* 5, no. 3 (Winter 1987): 359–90.

Jaynes, Julian. *The Origin of Consciousness in the Breakdown of the Bicameral Mind*. Boston: Houghton Mifflin, 1976.

Johnson, Roger. *Scores: An Anthology of New Music*. New York: Schirmer, 1981.

Mendel, Arthur. "Hans T. David (1902–1967)." *Journal of the American Musicological Society* 21, no. 3 (Autumn 1968): 407–9.

Miller, Leta E. "ONCE and Again: The Evolution of a Legendary Festival," in liner notes to *Music from the ONCE Festival, 1961–1966*. New World Records 80567-2, 2003.

Nyman, Michael. *Experimental Music: Cage and Beyond*. Cambridge: Cambridge University Press, 1974.

Pop, Iggy. *I Need More*. Los Angeles: 2.13.61 Publications, n.d.

Rancont, Ted. "Coins, Balloons and Explosions Play Roles in ONCE Festival." *Ann Arbor News*, February 29, 1964.

Rowland, Ingrid D. *From Heaven to Arcadia: The Sacred and the Profane in the Renaissance*. New York: New York Review of Books, 2008.

Sabatini, Michael. "Mikhail Bakhtin and Performance." Ph.D. diss., New York University, 1994.

Sumner, M., K. Burch, and M. Sumner, eds. *The Guests Go in to Supper: Texts, Scores and Ideas of Seven American Composers: Ashley, Ono, Cage, Anderson, Amirkhanian, Peppe, Atchley*. Oakland: Burning Books, 1986.

Yates, Frances. *The Art of Memory*. Chicago: University of Chicago Press, 1966.

———. *Giordano Bruno and the Hermetic Tradition*. Chicago: University of Chicago Press, 1964.

Velikovsky, Immanuel. *Earth in Upheaval*. Garden City, N.Y.: Doubleday, 1955.

———. *Worlds in Collision*. Garden City, N.Y.: Doubleday, 1950.

Vigneras, L. A. "The Cartographer Diogo Ribeiro." *Imago Mundi* 16 (1962): 78.

ROBERT ASHLEY DISCOGRAPHY

Performers aside from Ashley are given where appropriate; some of Ashley's recordings are made entirely with electronic means or generated solely by Ashley himself.

in memoriam . . . CRAZY HORSE (symphony), on *Music from the ONCE Festival*, Advance Recordings, 1966.

Purposeful Lady, Slow Afternoon, on *Electronic Sound*, Mainstream MS-5010, 1971.

Private Parts (The Record), Lovely Music LP 1001, 1978; CD 1001, 1990.

Sonata: Christopher Columbus Crosses to the New World in the Niña,the Pinta, and the Santa Maria Using Only Dead Reckoning and a Crude Astrolabe, "Blue" Gene Tyranny, piano, on *Just for the Record*, LP 1062, 1979; CD 1062, 2008.

Interiors Without Flash, on *Big Ego*, Giorno Poetry Systems, GPS 012-013, 1979.

The Bar, from *Perfect Lives*, Lovely Music LP 4904, 1981.

Music Word Fire and I Would Do It Again (Coo Coo), on *The Lessons*, Lovely Music LP 4908, 1981.

Yellow Man with Heart with Wings, Lovely Music CD 1003, 1990.

Perfect Lives, Lovely Music CD 4917(3) (3 CDs), 1991.

Improvement (Don Leaves Linda), Elektra/Nonesuch 79289-2, 1992.

Odalisque, on *Full Spectrum Voice*, Thomas Buckner, baritone, Lovely Music CD 3021, 1991.

Factory Preset, on *A Chance Operation*, John Cage tribute, Koch International 3-7238-2 Y6x2, 1993.

eL/Aficionado, Lovely Music CD 1004, 1994.

Outcome Inevitable, on *Outcome Inevitable*, The Relache Ensemble, O.O. Discs OO#18, 1994.

The Producer Speaks, on *Sign of the Times*, Thomas Buckner, baritone, Lovely Music CD 3022, 1994.

Van Cao's Meditation, on *With and Without Memory*, Lois Svard, piano, Lovely Music CD 3051, 1994.

Love Is a Good Example [from *The Immortality Songs*], on *A Confederacy of Dances*, vol. 2, Einstein Records EIN 003, 1995.

Automatic Writing, *Purposeful Lady Slow Afternoon*, and *She Was a Visitor*, Lovely Music CD 1002, 1996.

Atalanta (Acts of God), Lovely Music CD 3301, 1997.
in memoriam . . . KIT CARSON (opera) (excerpt), on *Ten Years of Essential Music*, Monroe Street, MSM 60101, 1997.
Your Money My Life Goodbye, Lovely Music CD 1005, 1999.
String Quartet Describing the Motion of Large Real Bodies and *How Can I Tell the Difference?* Alga Marghen CD1, 1999.
The Wolfman, Alga Marghen CD2, 1999.
Dust, Lovely Music CD 1006, 2000.
In Sara, Mencken, Christ and Beethoven There Were Men and Women, Lovely Music CD 4921, 2002.
in memoriam . . . CRAZY HORSE (symphony), Sonata, The Fourth of July, Details (2b), Fives, and *Quartet*, on *Music from the ONCE Festival, 1961–1966*, New World Records 80567, 2003.
The Fox, The Wolfman, The Wolfman Tape, and *The Bottleman*, on *Wolfman*, Plana-A 20NMN.048, 2003.
Perfect Lives, Lovely Music DVD 4917 2005.
Celestial Excursions, Lovely Music CD 1007, 2005.
Foreign Experiences, Lovely Music CD 1008, 2006.
Now Eleanor's Idea, Lovely Music CD 1009, 2007.
Tapdancing in the Sand, including *in memoriam . . . ESTABAN GOMEZ*, Ensemble MAE, Unsounds 15U, 2007.
Concrete, Lovely Music CD 1010, 2008.
Atalanta (Acts of God) II (Empire, Au Pair, The Etchings), Lovely Music CD 3303, 2010.

Filmography

Dr. Chicago (three films by George Manupelli), George Manupelli Films, 2006.
Music with Roots in the Aether, Lovely Music, 1976 (VHS), n.d. (DVD).

INDEX

1750 Arch, 77–78

Adams, John: *The Death of Klinghoffer*, 127; *Nixon in China*, 127
American Composers Orchestra, 111
AMM, 32
Ammons, Albert, 10
Ann Arbor, 7–8, 22
Aranovsky, Mark, 109
Arch Ensemble, 77–78
art of memory (Bruno), xi, 88–89, 94, 98
Ashley, Alvah J. (grandfather), 8, 135 (chap. 2, n. 3)
Ashley, Alvah J. "Cy" (uncle), 8, 9
Ashley, Diane (sister), 9, 12
Ashley, Mary (née Tsaltas, first wife), 17, 18, 27, 43, 45, 48, 78
Ashley, Robert: army experience, 17–18; conception of opera, 1–2, 57–61. *See also entries for specific works*
Ashley, Sam (son), 18, 60, 78, 80, 87, 97, 113, 115, 118, 121, 125–26
Ashley, Sarah (grandmother), 8
Ashley, Ward J. (father), 8, 9–10, 15
Atalanta (Ashley), x, 4, 5, 8, 57, 58, 61, 77–86, 87, 99
Austin, Larry, 34
Automatic Writing (Ashley), 53, 55–56

Babbitt, Milton, 24
Bach, Johann Sebastian, 4, 14–15; *Musical Offering*, 89
Bassett, Leslie, 14, 21
Beckett, Samuel, 123
Beethoven, Ludwig van, 4
Behrman, David, 28–29, 51–52, 54; *Runthrough*, 29
Berg, Alban, 14; Chamber Concerto, 16–17; Violin Concerto, 21
Berio, Luciano, 22, 26
Berlioz, Hector, 114
Bertoni, Nick, 47, 100, 124
Bhatt, Krishna, 55
Bischoff, John, 48
Bloomberg, (Mayor) David, 116
Bob Wills Band, "Milk Cow Blues," 122
Borkin, Harold, 20
Bottleman, The (Ashley), 26, 30, 116
Boulez, Pierre, 14, 24, 77
Brickman, Lawrence, 80
Bruno, Giordano, xi, 64, 88–89, 92–94, 96, 101, 121, 122
Buckner, Thomas: Ashley commissioned by, 111–12, 113; joins Ashley's ensemble, 77–78; operas performed, 80–83, 87–88, 96–97, 115, 117, 118, 121, 125
Budd, Harold, 32

Cacioppo, George, 21, 22
Cage, John, x, 5, 22, 24, 28, 32, 43, 50, 61; *4'33"*, 24; *Indeterminacy*, 22; *The Seasons*, 111
Cao, Van, 113
Castaneda, Carlos, 100–101
Celestial Excursions (Ashley), x, 13, 54, 116, 121–24

Christopher Columbus Crosses to the New World . . . (Ashley). *See* Piano Sonata (Ashley, 1959)
Cicero, 114
Cohen, Milton, 20
Combination Wedding and Funeral (Ashley), 72
Complete with Heat (Ashley), 32
conceptualism, 24–25
Concrete (Ashley), 5, 15, 116, 124–26
Conlon, Anne Ward (sister), 9, 10, 13
Coolidge, Elizabeth Sprague, 46
Cope, David, ix

David, Hans T., 14–15, 89
Davies, Dennis Russell, 114
Davies, Robertson, 4
DeMarinis, Paul, 48, 49, 53
DeMille, Richard, 100
Details (Ashley), 35–36
Dust (Ashley), x, 5, 8, 12–13, 18, 72, 99, 116–21

eL/Aficionado (Ashley), 60, 96–99, 103, 104, 110, 111, 113
Eliot, T. S., 15
Ellington, Duke, 3
Ensemble MAE, 111, 112, 114–15, 126
Entrance, The (Ashley), 38
Ernst, Max, 50, 79; *Une Semaine de Bonté*, 85

Fancy Free (*It's There*) (Ashley), 41–42, 48
Farley, Bill, 51
Fast Forward, 48
Feldman, Morton, 24–25, 32, 36, 38, 48
Finney, Ross Lee, 14, 18–19, 20, 136 n. 29
Fishburne, Mary S., 15
Fitzgerald, Kit, 76
Fives (Ashley), 36
Fluxus, 24
Foreign Experiences (Ashley), 1, 5, 8, 20, 47, 54, 59–61, 83, 99–104, 113
Fourth of July, The (Ashley), 26, 30, 36
Fox, The (Ashley), 29–30

Gena, Peter, x, 55
Gerhard, Roberto, 20–22; *Collages* (Symphony No. 3), 22
Glass, Philip, 51–52; *Akhnaten*, 127; *Einstein on the Beach*, 51, 127; *Satyagraha*, 127; *The Voyage*, 127
Gordon, Peter, 65, 76
Gurdjieff, George, 124

Hamilton, Tom, 82, 90, 121, 125
Hariton, Monya, 96
Hariton, Theodore (Ted), 9
Harrison, Lou, 47, 111
Haubenstock-Ramati, Roman, 32
Held, Barbara, 110–11
Hesiod, 2
Hidden Similarities (Ashley), 111, 126
Hitchcock, H. Wiley, 15, 31
Holm-Hudson, Kevin, 63–64, 139 (chap. 5, n. 7)
Homer, 2
How Can I Tell the Difference? (Ashley), 50
Humbert, Jacqueline: joins Ashley's ensemble, 78; operas performed, 60, 80–85, 87, 97, 113, 115, 117, 118, 124, 125
Hunt, Jerry, x

Ideas from the Church (Ashley), 103–4
"Immortality Songs, The" (Ashley), 110
Improvement: Don Leaves Linda (Ashley), x, 5, 6, 60, 61, 75, 90–96, 99, 101–2, 110
in memoriam . . . CRAZY HORSE (symphony) (Ashley), x, 32, 33–35, 60
in memoriam . . . ESTEBAN GOMEZ (quartet) (Ashley), 32, 33–35
in memoriam . . . JOHN SMITH (concerto) (Ashley), 32, 33–34
in memoriam . . . KIT CARSON (opera) (Ashley), 33–34, 104
In Sara, Mencken, Christ, and Beethoven There Were Men and Women (Ashley), 48–50
Ives, Burl, 29
Ives, Charles, 127

Jacobs, Paul, 26
Jaynes, Julian, *The Origin of Consciousness in the Breakdown of the Bicameral Mind*, 73
Johnson, Dickie, 10
Johnson, George, 65
Johnson, Mimi, 50–51, 53–56, 99, 127

Joyce, James, 2, 15
Joy Road Interchange (Ashley), 27

Kaplan, Wilfrid, 26, 43
Keller, Homer, 14
Kittyhawk (Ashley), 27, 42–43
Klein, Adam, 95
Klein, Howard, 47, 51
Kroesen, Jill, 65, 67, 75
Krumm, Philip, 27–28

La Barbara, Joan, 29; joins Ashley's ensemble, 90; operas performed, 87, 107, 108, 113, 115, 117, 118, 121, 125–26
Lahti, Uolevi, 22
Le Carré, John, 4, 97, 127
Leonard, Elmore, 127
Lewis, Lux Meade, 10
Liddell, Cynthia, ix, 39, 43
Lockwood, Annea, 24
lowriders, 104–9
Lovely Music label, 26, 54–55
Lucier, Alvin, 28–29, 32, 45, 51; *I Am Sitting in a Room*, 28; *Vespers*, ix, 29
Lyon, Margaret, 47

Machover, Tod, *Valis*, 127, 128
Makanna, Philip, 51–52, 54
Mamlok, Ursula, 16
Manhattan School of Music, 15–16
Manupelli, George, 17, 22, 43, 78; *Dr. Chicago*, 44–45, 98
Martinez, Dennis, 105
Medina, Arthur "LowLow," 107
memory, art of (Bruno), xi, 88–89, 94, 98
Milhaud, Darius, 46–47
Miller, Henry, 2–3
Mills College, 19, 44, 46–48, 53–54
minimalism, 24–25
Monteverdi, Claudio, 2, 5
Moorman, Charlotte, 37
Morton Feldman Says (Ashley), 48
Mumma, Gordon, 19, 20, 22, 28–29, 42, 50, 51–52; *Hornpipe*, 29
Munkasci, Kurt, 54
Musica Elettronica Viva, 32
Music with Roots in the Aether (Ashley), 51–53
Music Word Fire and I Would Do It Again (Coo Coo) (Ashley), 4, 75–76

Night Train (Ashley), 43
Nono, Luigi, 28
Now Eleanor's Idea (opera), 60–61, 83, 104–9, 120
Now Eleanor's Idea (tetralogy), 4, 57, 61, 69, 87–109, 117
Nyman, Michael, ix

Oliveros, Pauline, 32, 45, 46, 51, 77
ONCE festivals, 4, 7, 20, 22–29, 42–44
ONCE Group, 42–45, 60–61, 72
Outcome Inevitable (Ashley), 36, 110, 112–13

Paik, Nam June, 24
Partch, Harry, 2, 47
Paxton, Steve, 45
Payne, Maggi, 47
Perfect Lives (Ashley), x, 3, 4, 5, 10–11, 54–55, 57–75, 79, 87, 98, 99, 103–4, 105, 117, 122, 128–29
performance novels, 2
Performing Artservices, 50
Pesle, Bénédicte, 50
Peterson, Gordon, 19–20
Piano Sonata (Ashley, 1959), 25–26, 60, 99
Pop, Iggy, 28
Pound, Ezra, *Portrait d'Une Femme*, 83
Public Opinion Descends upon the Demonstrators (Ashley), 30–31, 61, 96
Purposeful Lady Slow Afternoon (Ashley), ix, 29, 38–40, 103

Quicksand (Ashley), 90, 127
Quintana, Julian, 105

Reich, Steve, 24; *Music for 18 Musicians*, 106
Relache ensemble, 110
Reynolds, Ann LaRee (aunt), 8
Reynolds, Floy E. Lewis (grandmother), 8, 10
Reynolds, Leon (uncle), 8
Reynolds, Nancy (mother), 8–9
Reynolds, Roger, 19, 21, 22, 26, 46–47

Reynolds, Rosalie (aunt), 8
Reynolds, Thomas (uncle), 8
Reynolds, Thomas Mann (grandfather), 8
Reynolds, Willard (uncle), 8–9, 79, 96
Riegger, Wallingford, 16
Riley, Terry, 24, 51
Rosenboom, David, 54, 78
Rouse, Mikel, 57; *Dennis Cleveland*, 128; *The End of Cinematics*, 128; *Funding*, 128
Rzewski, Frederic, 28

Sabatini, Arthur, 2
Sanborn, John, 65, 75–76
Schoenberg, Arnold, 23–24
serialism, 23–25, 32
She Was a Visitor (Ashley), x, 38–41, 103
Shorr, Paul, 80
Sinding, Christian, *Rustle of Spring*, 11
Sindona, Michele, 115
Smith, Ozzie, 124
Sonami, Laetita, 48
Sonic Arts Union, ix, 29, 32
Source magazine, ix, 33–34
Space Theater, 20, 21, 28, 44
Stevens, Wallace, 112
Stockhausen, Karlheinz, 5, 14, 22, 24, 34; *Klavierstücke*, 25
Stravinsky, Igor, 4
String Quartet Describing the Motion of Large Real Bodies (Ashley), 50
Superior Seven (Ashley), 110–12, 113, 114
Svard, Lois, 110, 113

Tanning, Dorothea, 50, 100
Tap Dancing in the Sand (Ashley), 111, 114–15
That Morning Thing (Ashley), 4, 27, 38–41, 42, 122
Tibetan Book of the Dead, The, 64–65, 67, 70
Title Withdrawn (Ashley), 52–53
Tourette's Syndrome, 53, 71
Tract (Ashley), 111, 112, 113
Trial of Annie Opie Wehrer, The (Ashley), 27, 43–44
Trio I (Ashley), 32
Tudor, David, 22, 24, 43
Turner, Joe, 10
Twain, Mark, 103
Tyranny, "Blue" Gene, x, 47; in Ashley's operas, 53, 63–76, 80–82, 96–97, 104; music by, 57; on the ONCE festival, 27–28, 34; playing style in the operas, 3, 39–40, 54–55, 63–64, 80–82; as promoter of Ashley's music, 25

University of Michigan, 7, 10, 13–15, 18–20

Van Cao's Meditation (Ashley), 26, 36, 110, 113
Van Tieghem, David, 65, 76
Vasulka, Woody, 114
Velikovsky, Immanuel, 101
Vriezen, Samuel, 137 n. 17

Wagner, Richard, 2; *Die Meistersinger*, 108; *The Ring of the Nibelungs*, 105; *Tannheuser*, 108
Waiting Room (Quartet) (Ashley), 32, 38
Waldrop, Keith, 48–49
Wehrer, Anne, 26, 27, 28, 43–44
Wehrer, Joseph, 20, 26, 27, 43
Wessel, David, 77
What She Thinks (Ashley), 52–53
When Famous Last Words Fail You (Ashley), 110, 111, 113–14
Wizard of Oz, The (movie), 54
Wolff, Christian, 28
Wolfman, The (Ashley), ix, 36–38, 78
Wolfman Tape, The (Ashley), 36
Wolgamot, John Barton, *In Sara, Mencken, Christ, and Beethoven There Were Men and Women*, 48–50

Yates, Frances: *The Art of Memory*, 64, 114; *Giordano Bruno and the Hermetic Tradition*, 64
Yellow Man with Heart with Wings (Ashley), 4, 99, 104, 110
Young, La Monte, 24, 32
Your Money My Life Goodbye (Ashley), 4, 5, 83, 110, 115–16

AMERICAN

Composers

Lou Harrison
Leta E. Miller and Fredric Lieberman

John Cage
David Nicholls

Dudley Buck
N. Lee Orr

William Grant Still
Catherine Parsons Smith

Rudolf Friml
William Everett

Elliott Carter
James Wierzbicki

Carla Bley
Amy C. Beal

Christian Wolff
Michael Hicks and Christian Asplund

Robert Ashley
Kyle Gann

KYLE GANN is an associate professor of music at Bard College and the author of several books, including *Music Downtown: Writings from the Village Voice* and *No Such Thing as Silence: John Cage's 4′33″*.

The University of Illinois Press
is a founding member of the
Association of American University Presses.

University of Illinois Press
1325 South Oak Street
Champaign, IL 61820-6903
www.press.uillinois.edu